playful

peg loom

weaving

A modern approach to the ancient
technique of peg loom weaving,
plus 17 projects to make

"To stimulate creativity, one must develop childlike inclination for play and the childlike desire for recognition" – Albert Einstein

playful

peg loom

weaving

A modern approach to the ancient
technique of peg loom weaving,
plus 17 projects to make

STÉPHANIE FRADETTE

WHITE OWL

To my beautiful girls, Sienna & Eva,
whose creative spirits inspire me everyday.

First published in Great Britain in 2022 by
PEN & SWORD WHITE OWL
An imprint of Pen & Sword Books Ltd
Yorkshire – Philadelphia

Copyright ©Stéphanie Fradette, 2022
www.lepetitmoose.com @lepetitmoose

ISBN 9781526793058

Group Publisher: Jonathan Wright
Series Editor and Publishing Consultant: Katherine Raderecht
Art Director: Jane Toft
Editor: Katherine Raderecht
Photography: Jesse Wild & Stéphanie Fradette
Illustrations: Laura Bremner

Printed and bound in the UK, by Short Run Press Limited, Exeter.

Pen & Sword Books Ltd incorporates the Imprints of Pen & Sword Books
Pen & Sword Books Limited incorporates the imprints of Atlas, Archaeology, Aviation,
Discovery, Family History, Fiction, History, Maritime, Military, Military Classics, Politics,
Select, Transport, True Crime, Air World, Frontline Publishing, Leo Cooper, Remember
When, Seaforth Publishing, The Praetorian Press, Wharncliffe Local History, Wharncliffe
Transport, Wharncliffe True Crime and White Owl.

For a complete list of Pen & Sword titles please contact:
PEN & SWORD BOOKS LIMITED
47 Church Street, Barnsley, South Yorkshire S70 2AS, England
E-mail: enquiries@pen-and-sword.co.uk
Website: www.pen-and-sword.co.uk
or
PEN AND SWORD BOOKS
1950 Lawrence Rd, Havertown, PA 19083, USA
E-mail: Uspen-and-sword@casematepublishers.com
Website: www.penandswordbooks.com

FSC
www.fsc.org
MIX
Paper from
responsible sources
FSC® C014540

contents

introduction

'Can you make it?' As a child, this was my mother's tantalising challenge whenever I wanted something new. My early years would see our dining table spend the majority of its existence as host to a banquet of creative pursuits; it very rarely fulfilled its intended purpose of dining! Whether it was the changing of the seasons, holiday projects or learning new sewing skills, there were always exciting craft and design projects happening. She wanted her space to be a reflection of who she was and so all the objects surrounding us in our modest home were made with intention and purpose. Handmade touches created a personalised, nurturing and sustainable feeling to my childhood home. So, it was a few raw materials, a splash of thoughtful colour, a dash of patience and a sprinkling of passion that were the essential ingredients that sculpted my early years, inspired my own children's upbringing and set my future path.

Since then, I have tried a range of creative outlets in my life — from photography to painting — but discovering fibre arts, specifically weaving, has provided me with the perfect balance of playfulness and a meditative form of self-expression. Weaving has helped me feel more energised and allowed me to think outside the box and find new perspectives. It has helped alleviate any stress and anxiety by giving me the time and head space to rekindle my playful childhood spirit through the possibilities that the loom has provided me.

I discovered peg loom weaving a few years into my weaving journey when I came across this simple tool at my children's nursery. The children were learning to weave using ribbons and yarn to teach them pattern making skills and hand-eye coordination. What an amazing way to create a woven textile, I thought! I quickly did a bit of research and started to experiment with this wonderfully simple and primitive type of loom. A collection of colourful projects (and years!) later and here I am, ready to share my new found passion for the humble peg loom with the world.

From starting out by making your own peg loom to eventually weaving round pieces, you'll soon be experimenting, having fun and creating beautiful pieces quickly and easily. The beauty of peg loom weaving is that each project can be adapted to suit your personal style by simply changing the colours or type of fibres you use. If you only have a few hours in the evening, are gathering friends for a day of crafting or you're feeling more ambitious and have a weekend free, there's a project to fit. I hope that makes my book perfectly suited to the ebb and flow of a creative's lifestyle!

Stéphanie x

chapter one: tools & techniques

There is no easier way to weave a piece of textile than by using a few simple pieces of wood. In this chapter we will discover the different type of looms available on the market and how to make our own versions at home. We'll also learn how to set up our loom ready for weaving, look at the different yarns you can use and then work through some of the various weaving techniques to help get your creative weaving juices flowing.

peg looms

The history of the peg loom is unclear, as specific historical texts or references are difficult to find. Nevertheless, the simplicity and portability of the peg loom means it was probably used from the Neolithic period. Because peg looms didn't need the wool to be spun or treated first (you can weave from raw sheep fleece) and were simple to make, they were used to produce wool textiles like coverlets, seat pads and rugs for centuries. I believe it is important to keep this ancient technique alive by encouraging makers and artisans to use, produce and pass on their skills to a wider community.

The unassuming peg loom has changed very little in style from its ancient origins. They all consist of multiple pegs with small holes drilled on one end to accommodate a string warp. The pegs are held in a supporting structure, normally a wooden board. This board rests securely on a table or clamped between two pieces of wood to hold the pegs, and acts as a rigid support onto which you will weave the main panels to create your chosen project.

The size of the board and pegs and the distance between the pegs are the main differences you will come across when looking for a shop-bought peg loom. Many models will offer a variety of width options. You can make or buy a loom with a single row of pegs in one size, or variants that offer multiple peg sizes and spacing options to choose from.

MAKING YOUR OWN PEG LOOM

I first started experimenting with peg loom weaving on a shop bought loom. When I shared my new found creative tool with my crafty mother, the first thing she said was: 'I can easily make one of those!' It worked perfectly, so I have been using her design ever since.

The width of your loom is based on the project and the space you have available. Most projects in this book have been created on a 50cm wide loom with 9mm pegs spaced 20mm apart. This is the most versatile width for most yarns in the book. If you are working with fleece or thick roving, make a second row of holes on the same board using 9mm pegs at 25mm intervals.

EXAMPLES OF STANDARD WIDTHS AND PEG SIZES.
6mm peg holes at 12mm spacing – thinner wool (UK 4 ply, DK or Worsted)
9mm peg holes at 20mm spacing – thicker wool (UK Chunky or Super Chunky)
9mm peg holes at 25mm spacing – chunky yarn, roving or fleece

---

Materials

- 9mm round dowels (should equate to a total length of 3600mm which is long enough to give you 24 x 15cm pegs)

- Wood block of the width and length of your choice (I've used a 46mm x 25mm x 500mm)

- 9mm & 2.5mm drill bit with drill

- Fine sanding paper

- Vice grip (helps to drill the dowel holes)

- Masking tape

- Mitre box (optional)

MAKING YOUR OWN PEG LOOM

1. Cut the 9mm dowel into smaller 15cm pegs — use a mitre box to hold everything in place while sawing.

2. Secure each peg in a vice grip or between 2 pieces of wood held by G-clamp. Next, drill a 3mm hole, at a distance of 30mm from the end of each peg. These holes will hold your warp. Lightly sand down both sides of the hole to remove any debris.

3. Using a ruler, mark the wood block at 20mm intervals in a straight line. If you have chosen to work with a 500mm length, this should give you 24 holes to drill.

4. To ensure you drill to the correct depth mark the drill with a piece of masking tape approx. 20mm from the tip of the bit. This will act as a guide and prevent you from drilling through the board! Once you have drilled the hole, give the surface a light sand.

5. It is now time to insert the pegs and ensure everything fits. A bit of resistance is okay, as you don't want your pegs to be wobbly while you work. If there is too much resistance, go back with the drill and give the hole a twirl or lightly sand the end of the peg. But not too much!

You can also use straws to replace the wooden sticks in the garland, necklace or coaster projects. Copper sticks are used for delicate projects such as earrings, necklaces and brooches.

weaving sticks

Whether you are using purpose–built weaving sticks or you make your own using a few straws, the end results will be similar; the perfect portable tools for on–the–go weaving! The number of sticks used for any particular project depends on the width of your finished piece. Don't work with too many at once as it can begin to get tricky to hold them all in one hand. However, there are purpose–built wooden clamps specifically designed to allow you to hold and work with a larger number of sticks. Personally, if I were planning to use more than 5 sticks, I would favour using the peg loom.

Smaller (copper or metal) weaving sticks are used for detailed work and will give a finer look to your finished piece. The 3mm copper sticks used in this book let us work with smaller yarn weights, such as 4 ply or DK yarns to create delicate pieces. Using a few extra warps gives extra-added stiffness to some of the accessories.

MAKING YOUR OWN WEAVING STICKS

1. Wooden sticks — Cut a 6-9mm wood dowel into equal lengths of approx. 2cm. Using a 2.5mm drill bit, create a small hole approx. 20mm from the end of the stick in order to accommodate the warp. Repeat this process for each stick and then sand down all the ends. If you don't have wooden sticks, **chopsticks** make another great option; they can be transformed by simply drilling a small hole into the flat end.

Using **straws** is an inexpensive and easy way to get started and a great way to get the children involved with creating their first project.

2A. Thread a single yarn (which will act as a warp) through the middle of the straw, which may be paper, wooden or metal. Next, tape one end of yarn to the outer extremity of the straw. Allow the longer warp to hang loosely from the other end.

2B. Tie your chosen yarn and begin weaving your pattern. Use your stitch of choice exactly as you would if using regular weaving sticks

2C. When you've reached the desired length of weaving, cut the warp free from each straw, pull it through the weaving and tie off using your choice of finishing method.

techniques

GETTING STARTED

Grab a cuppa and make yourself comfortable while you set up the peg loom on a table, preferably at waist height. You can either work with the warps (the vertical supporting yarns) in front of you or at the back of the loom, depending on the size of your project.

Choosing the right peg loom will depend on the finished width of your woven project, whist selecting the correct peg size and spacing will also vary on the type of fibres you are working with. It is important to note that narrow peg spacing will normally accommodate thinner yarn and a wider peg spacing is best for chunky yarns or fleece. If you're unsure, do a small test swatch, using different pegs and spacing. This will give you an idea of how the final piece will look, and help in deciding which peg set up works best.

WARPING YOUR LOOM

Before you begin weaving, you need to warp your loom. The **warp** (or core yarn) are the vertical supporting threads or yarns that are attached to your loom and will hold your **weft** (the fibres or materials you will use to weave with) in place. Keep in mind that in most cases, the warp will not be visible, as it will be covered by the weft, which is what provides the wonderful colours and textures that comprise your final piece.

The warp thread on a peg loom or weaving sticks always needs to be doubled up. Keep this in mind when calculating the length of warp needed for your project. Below is a simple formula to ensure you always have enough warp length on either side to tie off. This prevents your hard work from falling off when pushed down the warp. You may need to add warp if you plan on making the warp ends a feature, by leaving them as a fringe for example. Note: Circular weaving has a different method of calculating warp length. See page 26 for details.

Length of woven piece + 40cm (approx. 20cm on either end) x 2 = length of warp to cut x number of pegs

The simplicity and accessibility of the peg-loom is in the ease of it's warping methods

WHAT WARP TO CHOOSE?

If you are creating a piece that will be used and abused, such as a rug, then a stronger warp will be essential. Ideally the warp should not stretch or break when pulled such as a cotton string, twisted or linen yarn. I personally find that matching your warp to your project in terms of yarn weight and colour produces much better results in terms of the look and feel of your piece. This is especially so when creating cushions and scarves.

NOTE All these warping and weaving techniques are applicable to both weaving on a peg loom and with the weaving sticks. In some of the projects such as the woven necklace (page 54) and the bookish bookmark (page 58), I've chosen to use double warps on each of the pegs. This is because I want to fill in the 'tunnels' and add rigidity to the piece. Alternatively, in projects such as the coastal coasters (page 42) and the statement earrings (page 46), I've removed one of the warps to ease the finishing process and remove some of the bulk.

WARPING THE PEGS

There are several ways of securely attaching the warps to the peg loom or to your weaving sticks. I like using the leash method, as it is the most versatile way of attaching thicker warps. The choice of attachment type depends on several factors including personal taste, materials used to warp the loom and the final project that you wish to create.

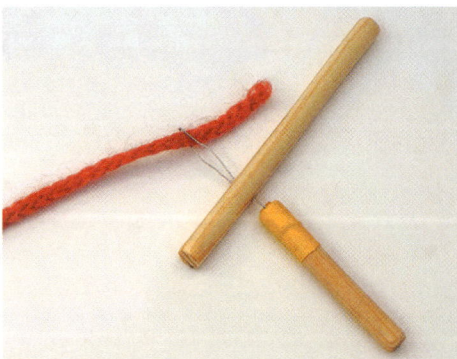

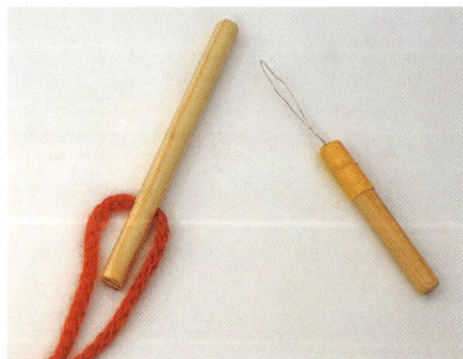

A. CLASSIC METHOD

Feeding your warp directly through the peg hole is the original and easiest method. Simply pull a threader (use a specific threading tool, wire or needle) through the peg hole, grab your string or yarn and pull it back through the hole. Pull and centre the doubled warp in the middle of the peg.

B. LOOPED PEGS

The looped method is useful for projects that will require a dowel to be inserted on the top of the piece as, for example, with a wall hanging. This works best when using a thinner warp as using a thick warp may catch during the weaving process. This technique can also be used if you are planning on adding tassels or Rya knots on the end of a cushion or rug. These can be secured onto the looped warp threads to secure the ends. This warping technique could be used instead of the leash method for the waves wall hanging on page 76.

C. LEASH METHOD

I suggest using the versatile leash method when using a thicker warp that cannot be threaded directly through the peg holes.

The leashes are small 10–15cm lengths of thin string attached through the peg holes to create a small loop. The leash is then tied off with an overhand knot. The warp itself is secured to each leash using a lark's head knot, either on the leash or around the peg, as shown.

WEAVING TECHNIQUES

A huge advantage of working with the peg loom is that the rigid open-top weaving pegs allow for quick weaving in and out of each peg. You can also work directly from the yarn ball. Many traditional tapestry weaving techniques can be replicated on the peg loom, albeit with a little less refinement and precision because you do not retain the same weft/warp tension as a heddle loom or a frame loom, once the fibres have been pushed off the stiffness of the pegs. *When 'rows' are described, this refers to two weft (yarn) passes across the loom. For example: the first pass across the pegs will be from right to left, stopping at the peg where you want the colour to stop, followed by a reverse pass from left to right.*

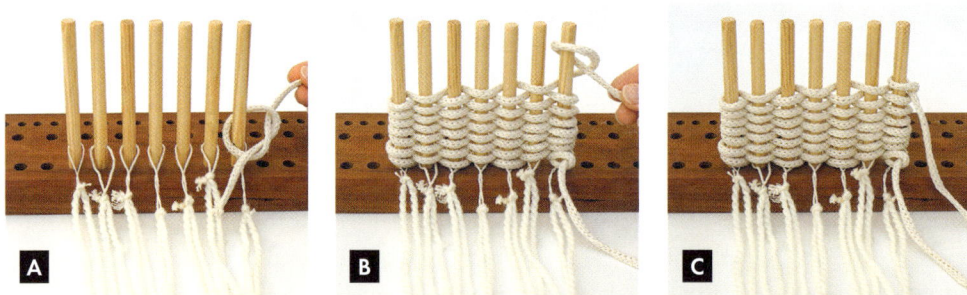

TYING ON & OFF

To attach the first yarn weft to the loom, I prefer to do a single overhand knot (A) to either the right or left outer peg. If you are using chunky yarns, use a half hitch knot (B) for tying on (or off) yarn ends (C). These will blend in more seamlessly when weaving ends in. When changing colour, tie off the yarn with your preferred knot and begin with a new colour. You can tie overhand knots that you simply untie when weaving ends in. Always leave a 7–10cm cut yarn end to ease the weaving and tidying-up process when the piece is completed.

PLAIN WEAVE

Plain weave is the most basic and simple of stitches. It consists of passing the yarn, also known as the weft, around alternating back and front pegs. When you reach the end of the row of pegs or where you wish the colour to stop, turn the yarn around in the opposite direction and repeat in the opposite pattern.

ANGLED SHAPE

Increasing and decreasing the weft to create shapes is a fundamental technique to take your patterns to the next level. Adding more yarn rows on the same peg will give you a sharper angle, whereas weaving a single row per peg before increasing or decreasing yarn rows will form a more obtuse angle to your shape. Play around with the slanted shapes using 1 to 3 rows per peg. To fill in the shape, copy the number of rows from your original pattern.

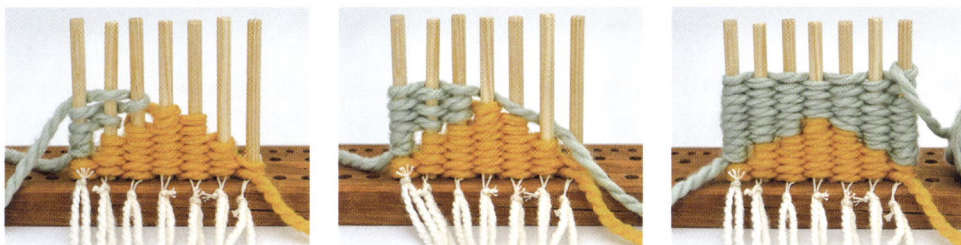

CURVED SHAPE

Start by deciding the curved shape you want to create. Weave the wider portions before reducing the number of pegs the yarn is wrapped around at each pass. A paper template placed behind the loom can guide your weaving to create your desired curve. It is easier to weave a single curve by filling the full height of the pegs before moving the yarn down the warps.

INTERLOCKING STITCH

This technique works well when you want to cleanly join colours as, for example, when weaving a steep diagonal or a vertical line. Start with a different colour at each end of the loom and weave them towards each other until they meet. Join the colours by crossing them in the space between 2 pegs, before weaving back in the return direction.

IRREGULAR HATCHING WEAVE

This technique is used to create either an illusion of colour blending or, alternatively, a series of lines through the piece. The irregular hatching weave is achieved by weaving two colours starting from opposing ends of the loom towards each other. They are then joined by crossing them between 2 pegs before going back in the opposite direction (as in the interlocking stitch example). Repeat by randomly alternating the pegs where the two colours meet in order to create a hatching effect.

SLIT

A vertical slit is created by weaving two colour blocks around adjoining pegs, without an interlock or sharing the same peg, when side–by–side. The vertical slit is useful for creating an intentional 'hole' in the woven fabric. This technique can be used to create a buttonhole or a keyhole for a scarf for example. Slits could also be used for experimental hangings or to insert sticks or dowels.

TWINING WEAVE

The twining stitch is often used in traditional weaving to 'lock in' plain weave, at the beginning or end of a piece. With peg loom weaving, it is an easy and decorative stitch to use throughout the process with a variety of materials.

If you are using a single colour, cut a long length of yarn, fold in half and wrap the middle loop around the peg you wish the twining to begin. The two strands will be interlaced together around each peg.

If using two colours, begin by securing each yarn colour around the same peg. Then begin interlacing both strands to create a twisted weave in the same direction.

SOUMAK WEAVE

The soumak weave or stitch is one of my favourites. It is also called the braided stitch when adding two or more rows of this kind in sequence. It is great to add texture, especially when using chunky yarns, roving or multiple yarns.

Attach the yarn where you wish the colour to start (in this case to the right peg) and bring over two pegs before drawing the yarn back behind and through one of the pegs. Repeat until you have reached the end and wrap the yarn twice around the last peg. Reverse the stitch to weave the second row, as shown.

REVERSE SOUMAK WEAVE

For the reverse soumak, simply bring the loop to the back of the weave instead of the front as per the regular soumak weave. Tie the yarn to the peg you want the colour to begin and bring the yarn behind the second peg and back to the front. Then wrap it behind two pegs. Repeat this process, ensuring every peg has a loop in the front. When you have reached the end peg, wrap around twice and continue in the same pattern, as shown.

Stitches and patterns can get really interesting when using a combination of soumak and reverse soumak rows. The cowl project on page 88 is a good example.

HORIZONTAL STRIPES

These stripes are easier than they look and quite satisfying with the right colour combination. Begin by tying the first colour and weaving one row before returning to the original position. Tie a second colour and weave a row. Take the yarn end from the first colour, bring in front of the peg whilst criss crossing the yarn end of the second colour. Continue to weave following the pattern, changing colour every time you reach the starting point.

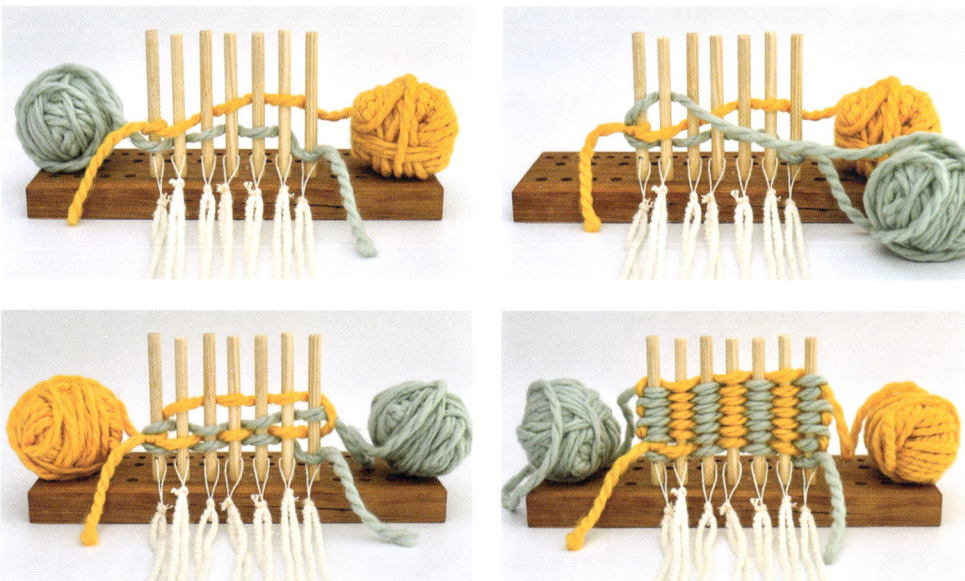

VERTICAL STRIPES

Also called 'pick and pick', this technique allows you to weave vertical lines of contrasting colours between two yarns. Attach the first colour to one side of the loom and weave one pass. Attach the second colour to the opposite side and weave one pass to the opposite side. Pick up your first yarn and hook it under the second colour (in this case the knot) and bring it to the front, continuing the pattern of over and under. Once you get to the other side, leave the yarn end, pick up the second colour and hook it in place behind the first yarn end to continue, as shown.

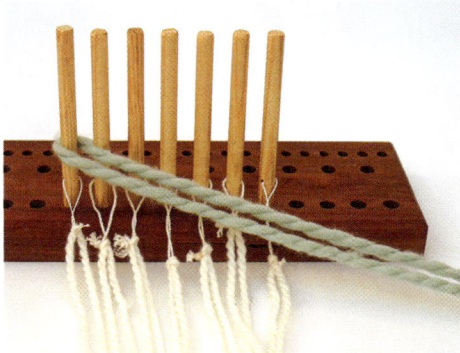

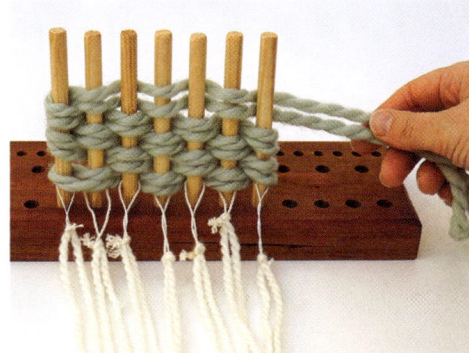

BASKET WEAVE

This subtle yet detailed weave works beautifully with chunky yarns or rope to really bring out the texture. Begin by cutting a length of yarn and folding it in half, effectively doubling the weft. Wrap the middle fold of the yarn around the first peg and weave in and out by stacking the two rows neatly one on top of the next. The bench cover on page 102 is a good example of this technique.

RYA KNOT

Rya knots are often used at the bottom of a wall hanging as fringe throughout the piece or to create a pile weave on the main woven panel. This knot is recommended for woven textiles that will not be manipulated. This is because a piece created on a peg loom can often have an overall looser tension than tapestry weaving, and so is best used for wall hangings or decorative cushions. Before any Rya knots are inserted, ensure you have at least 3–4 rows of plain weave to support the knots.

Begin by cutting 2 or 3 equal lengths of your preferred yarn. These will be folded in half, therefore calculate the length of the fringe x 2 plus add 3cm for the knot. Then wrap the folded bundle of yarns around 2 pegs. The ends will go between the two pegs, either under the fold or above it, as shown. Pull down tightly. After you have completed a row of Rya knots, weave at least 2–3 rows of plain weave to lock in the knots. Experiment with the number of yarns used, weight, colour combinations and yarn lengths.

ADVANCING THE WEFT

Peg Loom

Once approximately ¾ of the pegs have been filled with yarn and the final row of fibre has had a full pass over all the pegs, it is time to advance your weft down onto the warp strings. Starting from the left or right side, begin by gently removing the first peg from its hole, pull it upwards until you see the bottom of the peg and the warp has travelled through the weft 'tunnel'. Replace the empty peg in its original position on the board. Repeat this process until all the pegs have been pulled out and the woven weft is sitting below, securely held by the warp strings.

You may want to remove all the pegs from their holding space at once before replacing them one by one, once the warp has been pulled through. This method works for smaller pieces but I personally find this method comes with the risk of having the pegs criss-cross and you not placing them back in their correct position on the board. If not immediately rectified, this will cause the rest of the piece to not glide properly downwards when advancing the weft and will be noticeable in the finished textile.

Weaving Sticks

To advance the weft whilst using weaving sticks, begin by placing the sticks on a flat surface. While holding the weft on the sticks, begin pulling the sticks upwards one by one until you have exposed ¾ of the sticks. You do not need to pull them out completely to begin weaving the next section. If you are finished weaving, then pull the weaving sticks out completely, until you have at least 10-15cm of weft on both sides of the woven piece.

CIRCULAR WEAVING

Circular weaving is a truly magical way to create a piece that is bigger than the loom and beyond the rectangular limits that are often associated with a weaving. This technique of building wedges or pie segments on the peg loom will slowly produce a curved piece. Once the piece is off the loom and the warps are pulled, they will eventually come together to create a flat circle. When warps are pulled even more, you can construct a bowl or conical shape. This is a great opportunity to experiment with unique 3D woven results.

To create the pie wedges or segments, I've used a few different row combinations for each of the circular weaving projects.

Most of them require you to weave 2 to 3 rows on all of the pegs, before decreasing one peg at a time. Next, weave 2 to 4 rows across the pegs before decreasing again. Continue until you have only one peg to wrap around. Follow with a series of wedges until you have the desired circumference, by pushing down and pulling in the middle warp. The smaller pieces can take between 6–12 pie segments whereas larger pieces may require weaving up to 20–25 triangular sections.

There are no hard rules; experimenting will give you the best results. You will yield different results depending on peg thickness, yarn type and weight. Have fun with it!

HOW MANY PEGS TO USE?

In order to see how many pegs are needed to create your circular piece, you must first determine the diameter of the final round piece. Once this has been established, divide that number in half. This will be your radius. The radius will in turn inform the width of the pegs needed. As we are building triangular segments on the peg loom, one side of the pegs will have more rows built up. This will be the outer portion of the circle. The other side of the pegs will have fewer rows and this represents the middle part of your circle.

In some cases, I have used graded pegs specifically made to weave in the round. Similar results can be achieved with pegs that are the same length. You will simply have to slide the pie wedges (weft) down more often onto the warps strings.

WARPING FOR A CIRCULAR WEAVE

There is a little bit of calculation needed before beginning on a circular piece and this may need you to dig back to your early maths lessons!

First, longer warps are needed for the outer perimeter of your woven circle whilst shorter warps will be used for the centre of the circle. The best way to calculate the length of your longest warp is to apply the Pi formula (π)

1. Calculate the diameter of your piece, which is your radius x 2.

2. Diameter x 3.14 (π) = circumference of your finished circle.

3. Circumference x 2 + 40-50cm = length of outer warp + excess for tying off.

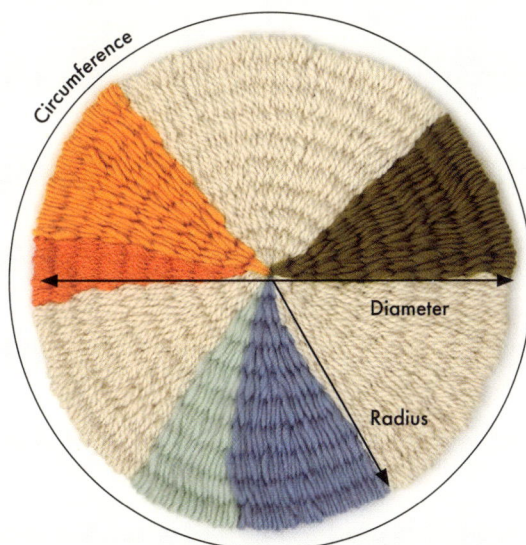

Each warped peg will be subsequently shorter than the outer warp, which is the longest. The centre warps should always be a minimum of 30cm to be safe. There are handy charts available online that can precisely calculate the amount of warp needed for each peg, when weaving a circle.

NOTE Remember, it doesn't need to be complicated! If a project requires too many precise mathematical calculations, simply cut all the warps the same length as the warp from the outer circumference (which will be the longest one) of the circle.

CLOSING THE CIRCLE

Once you have woven the desired number of pie wedges required for your piece, tying each warp with its opposing warp end will bring it all together. Pulling the warps at various tensions will either flatten your circular piece or make it a 3D object, such as the statement earrings (page 46).

To complete a circular piece, which will lay flat, such as the round seat pad (page 84), begin pulling the 2 centre warps ends tightly and tie off using a double knot. The first knots should remain quite loose to begin with, as you may need to return to them for adjustment. Move on to the next warp pair, working from the centre outwards. Adjust the circle by keeping the tension balanced in order for the circle to remain flat. Finish by weaving the warp ends into their appropriate tunnel (or channel) to conceal the join. Remember, it is easy to create a bowl, cone or any other 3D vessel simply by pulling the outer warp thread together tightly.

finishing off

Very much like other fibre-based weaving techniques, there is always some extra work needed to finish your piece after the creative enjoyment of weaving is done. The weft ends will need to be woven back in the fabric and the warp edging finished to lock your woven fabric in to prevent your piece from unravelling when in use and provide a professional finish to all your hard work. You may choose to manipulate the warp ends in a decorative way and I've shown you a few options below to take your creation to the next level.

OVERHAND KNOT

This is tying off the ends the easy way. Doing so in groups of 3 or more warps is the most straightforward method to lock in your piece. This is achieved by counting how many warp ends are hanging on either side of the fabric and tying them off in equal groups. Use overhand knots to ensure the weft stays in place. Just make sure you don't end up with 2 warps on either end! This works well in projects where the warp ends are hidden, like cushions.

DAMASCUS EDGE

This easy technique produces a braided-like knot, to cleanly finish the edging of your woven piece. Starting from the left (or reverse from the right), fold the left warp in a number '4' shape over the 2nd warp. It uses a half-hitch knot to tie off two adjoining warps in a 'over, under and up' motion. The knotted warp goes upwards and the remaining passive warp then becomes the new knotted warp. You can finish off with a half-Damascus (as pictured) or repeat in reverse for a second row to complete a full Damascus.

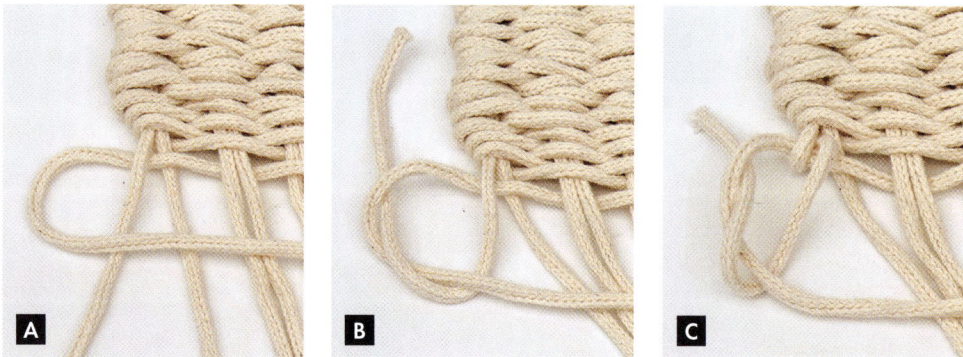

DOUBLE HALF-HITCH KNOT

Some of you might recognise the horizontal double half-hitch knot as belonging to the craft of macramé. For finishing a peg loom project, it makes for a secure and decorative finish. This is especially so when working with rope, jersey or any other thicker cotton yarn. The trick is to leave a yarn (weft) end from the first and last colour, which is the width of your woven piece + approximately 10cm. This will be used as the filler cord onto which each warp will be wrapped around twice, to create a horizontal bar as edging. It is easier if the lead cord is passed under the first warp and then brought back over the same warp (A). Then take the warp over the lead cord and through the loop (B), while holding the lead cord horizontally. Gently glide the knot upwards. Repeat for a second knot using the same warp (C). Repeat the two knots for each of the warps to create a horizontal bar locking in the work at the base of the weave. The trivet project on page 50 is a good example of this technique.

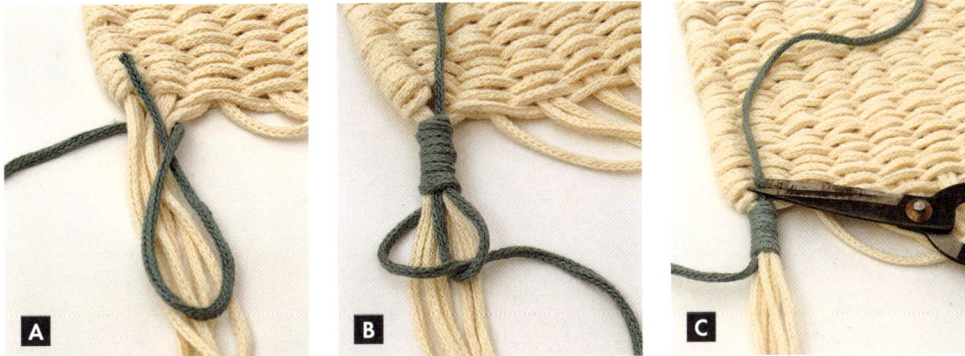

WHIPPING KNOT OR WRAP KNOT

This provides a fun way to tie off the warp ends if you are looking for a decorative finish to your rug, blanket or wall hanging. A length of yarn between 20–40cm is used to securely tie an equal group of warp ends. Loop the end in a small loop (A), then coil the yarn end around the bundle several times. Next, pass the yarn end through the loop (B), and pull it through behind the coil using the top yarn end. Cut the excess ends close to the base (C) and tuck excess in the coil using a blunt needle.

LOOPED ENDS

Using the peg loop method when warping will allow you to have loops on one side of your piece. You can use these loops to insert a rod or wooden dowel to hang your creation, as on the waves wall hanging (page 76). This can also work by cutting off the leashes and/or undoing the lark's head knot used whilst attaching the loop onto the string leashes. By using this technique, you could easily turn your piece around and attach a fringe to the loops using rya knots. This would be perfect for pieces that are intended to be hung by creating length and texture to your creation.

WEAVING ENDS IN

As you weave a panel on your peg loom, there will inevitably be yarn ends that will need to be tidied away to give a clean and professional finish to your piece. I recommend you complete this only once the weaving portion is done, with the warps pulled into position and tied off. If you attempt to weave the yarn ends in while you still have to move the woven panel up and down the warps, this may cause the yarn ends to pop back out. If you are weaving a circular piece or attaching both warp ends together, such as in the planter or cowl projects, again keep the task of weaving the ends for the last step of the project.

Using a large eyelet needle is an essential tool when it comes to easily finishing off the piece. A latch hook works well for chunkier yarns, dreadlock wool or rope. To be on the safe side and to ensure ends don't pop out when using your piece, weave them into their appropriate 'tunnel' and in a similar colour, at least 5–7cm inwards. Cut off near the base of the yarn end.

EXPERIMENTING WITH MATERIALS & COLOUR
Fibre Variations

With fibre arts gaining a loyal and worldwide following in the past few years, it is easy to see why so many amazing types of different fibres are now available to the craft community. From soft cotton ropes to felted yarns, all the way to colourful merino roving and lust-worthy core spun yarns, there are so many amazing choices for the fibre aficionado!

Although the history of the peg loom began by weaving with unspun fleece, treated and processed quality fibres definitely bring a fresh and modern appeal to this ancient technique. This was the goal when choosing the materials for this book and to show you ways to go beyond fleece and inject some contemporary flair into the craft. I just love working with chunky and textured fibres as you will see throughout this book. Feel free to experiment with doubling up the yarns, twisting them together or combining them for a unique take on the usual suspects.

Wool is not the only material that can be worked in and out of the pegs. Creating rag rugs has been a popular way to up-cycle strips made from old sheets or t-shirts. Why not unravel that old wool jumper and use the yarn? The possibilities are endless and the only limit is your imagination.

YARN GUIDE

UK	US	AUS
1 ply	Laceweight	2 ply
2 ply	Fingering	3 ply
3 ply	Sock	3 ply
4 ply	Sport	5 ply
DK	DK/ Light Worsted	8 ply
Aran	Worsted	10 ply
Chunky	Bulky	12 ply
Super Chunky	Super Bulky	14 ply

Experimenting with different
materials and colour
combinations is one of the
joys of weaving

HOW MUCH YARN TO USE?

Knowing how much fibre to purchase for a project is important, especially when you've found the perfect one–of–a–kind yarn. Just like knitting, crochet or tapestry weaving, creating a small sample swatch with the peg size, yarn weight and spacing you intend on using is the easiest method of working out how much you need. Then, either measure or weigh the unravelled yarn (weft) or weigh the sample piece including the warp.

For example:

10cm x 10cm sample of **chunky yarn** woven on 9mm pegs on chunky warp = approx. 14g
Total length of final woven piece = 100cm

10cm x 10cm = 14 g
100cm x 10cm = 140g

Add approximately 10-15% extra for contingency and, if using the same yarn for your warp, add that in as well by calculating the length (depending on what you are making).

DIFFERENT LOOMS

As you'll see throughout this book, projects are not limited to traditional peg looms. I have gone beyond and suggested smaller chopsticks and straws as weaving sticks all the way up to much larger wooden dowels, such as for the desert headboard project (page 110). Why not use your natural surroundings to get creative on your next outdoor adventure and find some sticks to weave with? Oh the possibilities!

The
Colour
Wheel

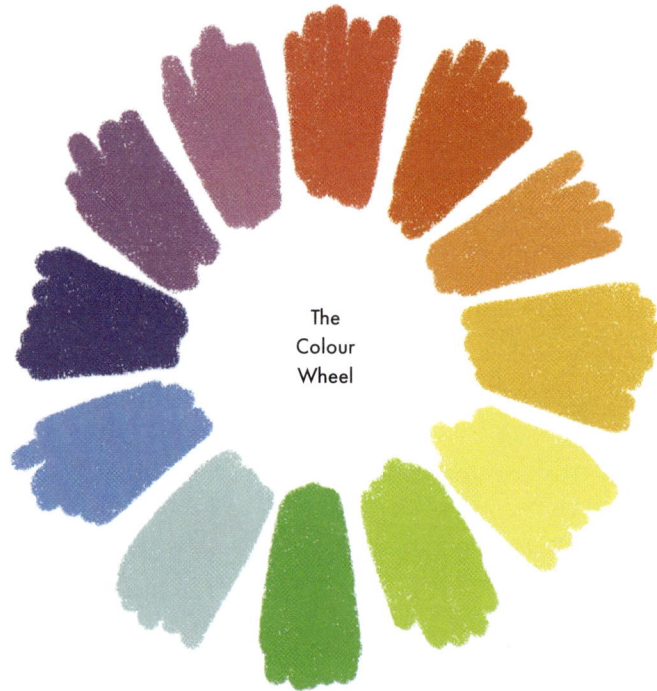

CRAFTING WITH COLOUR

There's a reason that blue and orange work so well together and that comes down to good old colour theory. Even after playing with colour for so many years, I still use my colour wheel to help me with combinations and not go astray when faced with a wall full of yarns! There are some amazing books and publications out there covering colour theory in detail and I highly recommend that you consult these if you wish to dive deeper in the fascinating world of colour. Although the basic rules of a balanced colour combination are rooted in the colour wheel, these rules are definitely not set in stone. With colourful maximalist and eclectic styles all over our social feeds, there's an abundance of unusual colour combinations popping up in interiors around the world. Pinterest is a great place to visit if you are looking for inspiration. From fibre crafts, illustrations or mood boards, you can easily draw out what colours make your heart sing.

That being said. here are a few basic rules and schemes to follow on your next project. Colour harmony always delivers good visual balance and is instantly pleasing to the eye.

Complementary colours

When in doubt, you can't go wrong with this colour combination. It is one of the strongest and consists of two colours directly opposite each other on the colour wheel.

Split complementary colours

The split complementary colour scheme is a variation of the complementary colour scheme but uses three colours. These are generally easier to use and have an intuitive approach. Begin with one colour base, then pair it with the two colours on either side to its complement.

Analogous colours

This is one of my favourites combinations to use and creates a strong visual and cohesive look. This is where you pick three colours adjacent to each other, which includes one dominant colour, usually a primary colour.

Monochromatic colours

This does not mean using black or white but rather using one colour in different tones, shades and tints to create a harmonious look in a piece. I find there is freedom in using only one hue to create beautiful gradient pieces.

Projects are planned around set time frames to fit comfortably into your daily life, including evening makes, creative day camps and weekend 'craftcations'

the projects

The projects in the following three chapters have all been thought out to ease you gently into the techniques according to how much time you have free during your week to dedicate to peg loom weaving.

In Chapter 2: Evening Makes, I designed the projects to be completed easily when you're winding down after a busy day. I wanted you to enjoy the satisfaction of finishing your make before going to bed. Because most projects are created using hand-held weaving sticks, they are also nicely portable, so you can craft while sitting in your favourite seat.

For Chapter 3: Creative Day Camp, grab your friends and get crafty together while creating projects that will make your homes even more beautiful. These projects may take only an afternoon, but if you include brunch then you can make it a full craft day camp!

Chapter 4: Weekend Craftcation features projects that can take up to a few days to complete, depending on your approach and the time you have available to play. These makes may be more labour intensive, such as the desert headboard, or time consuming like the modern clutch.

Whatever project you choose to make first, I guarantee it will deliver a satisfying result!

Projects are suitable for various skill levels from beginner to experienced. If you want to ease gently into peg loom weaving, the entry rug, statement necklace or the bookmark are great places to begin your journey. If you are feeling confident, there is nothing stopping you from tackling a more challenging project on your first attempt, such as the skyline cushion or the planter basket.

Remember, peg loom weaving is a pretty straightforward craft. With a little patience and time, you'll soon be on your way to enjoying all the benefits and satisfaction that weaving on a peg offers.

chapter two: evening makes

The series of projects in this chapter are perfect for that 'me time' after you've settled in for the evening with relaxing tunes and your drink of choice. You'll find that most of the makes are created using weaving sticks or on a small peg loom — perfect for weaving in your favourite cosy armchair. The trivet and the bookmark are great for experimenting with some of the techniques covered in Chapter 1 and all of the stitches are interchangeable. Have fun!

coastal coasters

I love that these versatile woven circles can take on various moods and styles depending on your chosen colours. The beauty of these coastal coasters is that each one is quickly made in under an hour so you can create one while relaxing and listening to your favourite podcast.

You will need

- 1 x coaster
- Weaving sticks — 4 sticks of approx. 10mm
- DMC Natura Cotton XL in Teal x 1 — Approx 20g
- DMC Natura Cotton XL in Light Blue x 1 — Approx 10g
- DMC Natura Cotton XL in Mustard x 1 — Approx 10g
- Weaving needle
- Scissors

Techniques
Circular Weaving

Difficulty
Intermediate

Warp
4 x 90cm

Finished piece
The coasters pictured have a diameter of 11cm. However, this will vary depending on size of weaving sticks, chosen materials and yarn type.

STÉPHANIE'S TIPS

- Keeping an even tension whilst weaving is key in producing a neat coaster. Holding the sticks quite closely together in your hand will help.
- Once finished, the process of weaving in the warp ends into the woven piece can be streamlined by removing one of the doubled warps from each tunnel.

43

1. Cut 4 lenghts of 90cm of your chosen warp, preferably choose a yarn colour you can hide between two pie segments of the same colour (first and last pie segments). Fold in half and thread through the hole of each stick using a threader or a weaving needle.

2. Using an overhand knot, attach the first colour on the right hand peg. Begin weaving between the pegs for 2 rows on all 4 sticks. Next, weave 3 rows on 3 sticks, 3 rows on 2 sticks and complete the first pie by weaving 3 rows around the last stick, as shown. Repeat for 2 other pie segments. Cut and tie off.

3. Continue weaving with a second colour, using the same technique for one pie segment only. Holding the woven sections, begin pulling each of the sticks to bring the warp through.

4. Continue adding pie segments as shown, for a total of 12 segments of your chosen colours.

You will see them all come together, in a semicircle, as they are taken off the sticks and warped cut from the sticks.

5. Take the warp strings and pull them so that they are equal lengths on both sides, pulling more from the centre outwards. Then, holding the woven piece, remove one of the warp strings from each pair, by pulling gently. This will make the coaster less bulky.

6. Beginning with the centre warps, tie off the warps with a double knot, joining them with their adjoining warps. Ensure you don't pull too tightly and the circle remains flat during the tying process.

7. Using a large eyelet tapestry needle, clean up all the loose ends by weaving them into their respective tunnels. Try and weave them as far in as possible, then cut off the excess yarn ends.

8. Time to make yourself a cuppa and repeat for your next coaster until you have a set.

statement earrings

These earrings are created using the smallest weaving sticks. You can adapt them to suit your style, depending on your fibre choice. The soft mercerized cotton yarn adds a nice sheen to them. You can omit the jellyfish–like tassels for a more structural look or change up the colours to match your favourite feel–good outfit.

You will need

- 6 x 3mm metal weaving sticks
- Scheepjes Catona in Shell, 4 ply — Approx. 15g
- Scheepjes Catona in Mustard, 4 ply — Approx. 10g
- Scheepjes Catona in Teal, 4 ply — Approx. 10g
- 2 x 6–8mm metal cap ends
- 2 x Jump rings
- 2 x Earwires
- Jewellery pliers
- Weaving needle
- Scissors

Techniques
Plain weaving + Circular Weaving

Difficulty
Intermediate

Warp
6 x 50cm

Finished piece
9cm long (with tassel) x approx. 4cm

1. Thread each of your weaving sticks with a 50cm long piece of yarn. I recommend using the same colour of at least 2 pie wedges. This will allow you to hide the joining knots seamlessly between these two wedges, as long as you start and finish with the same colour.

2. Holding the weaving sticks in one hand, slightly fanned out, tie an overhand knot with the first colour on the right hand peg. This will be the base of the cone.

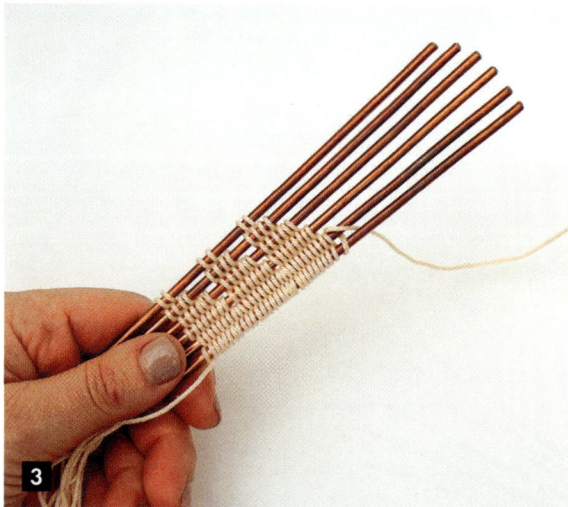

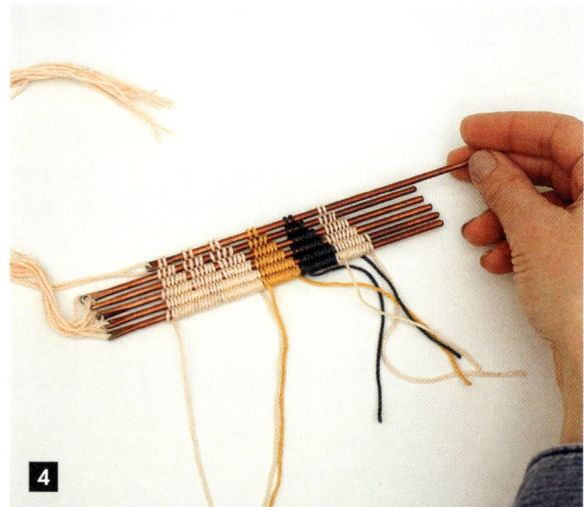

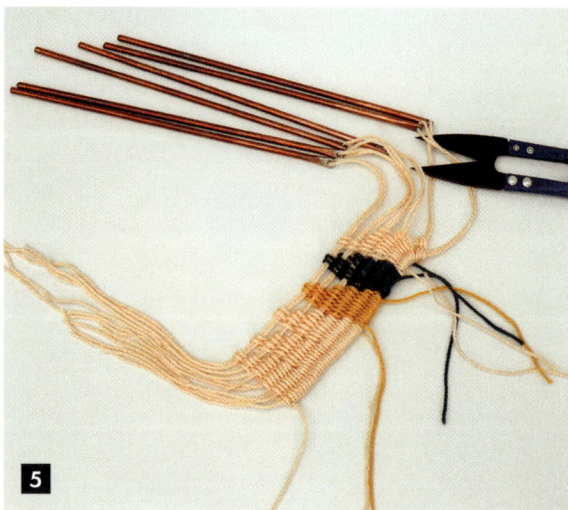

3. Begin weaving 2 rows across the 6 sticks before weaving 2 rows across 5 sticks, by dropping the left side stick. Followed by 2 rows across 4 sticks, 2 rows across 3 sticks and finishing the first pie wedge with 2 rows across 2 sticks. Weave 3 pie wedges of the same colour, before tying off, on the right hand side using an overhang or slip knot.

4. Using the picture as guide, continue with your chosen colours until you have 6 pie wedges. Remember to start and finish with the same colour as

your warp to hide the join.

5. Place your sticks on a flat surface and pull each stick out slightly so you have an equal amount of warp on either side of the woven sticks. Cut the warp off from the sticks.

6. You will have 2 warps going through in each tunnel. While holding the piece with one hand, gently remove one of the warp strings from each pair. This will keep things a little tidier when weaving the ends in and facilitate tying knots.

48

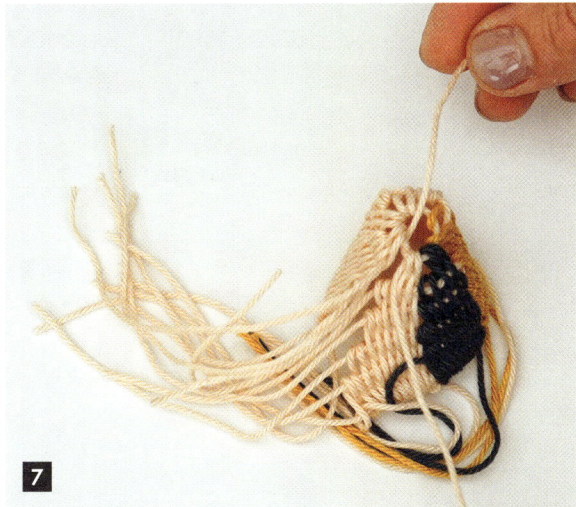

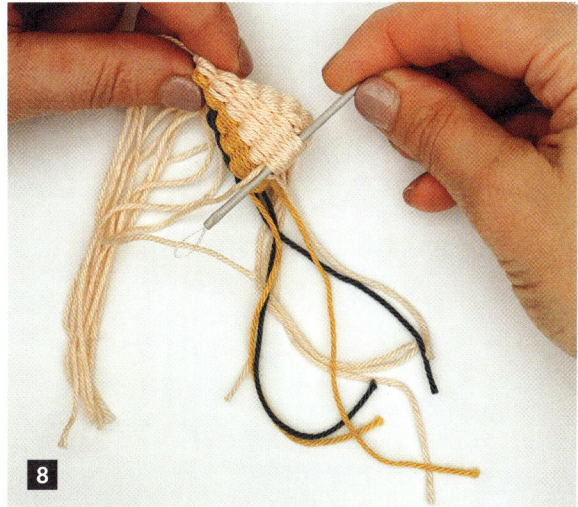

7. Start pulling the inner part of the earring together and tie the opposing warp end tightly using a double knot. Continue gradually until you have pulled in and tied off all of the adjoining warps of the same row together, forming a cone.

8. Now you need to tuck all the loose ends into the woven cone. Using a weaving needle, begin weaving in the ends at least 1cm into the 'tunnel'. Carefully cut excess yarn off. This is a meticulous process as there are so many ends in the way, but do it methodically to create a perfectly smooth little cone.

9. If adding a tassel, cut 12 ends of approx. 15cm and tie off in the middle of the bundle. With a needle, thread the centre thread and pull through the centre of the cone, along with a drop of Superglue and pull. Let the glue dry and cut extra yarn off.

10. Glue the end cap to the top of the earring; ensuring the top few rows are well tucked in. Attach a jump ring and ear wire. Repeat for the second earring.

49

rope trivet

This trivet project is a quick and easy one to get familiar with your peg loom. The geometric pattern is simple and effective — it would look great using a variety of stitches such as the vertical or horizontal lines. Using rope makes it extra cushy and is the perfect stylish resting place for a hot pot of tea.

You will need

- Peg loom of at least 30cm wide 9 x 9mm pegs
- Return of the Mac, 3mm Cord by Hobbycraft in Cream. Any 3mm cotton rope will suit this project. — Approx. 60g
- Return of the Mac, 3mm Cord by Hobbycraft in Mustard — Approx. 30g
- Weaving needle or crochet/latch hook
- Scissors

Techniques
Plain Weaving + Shaping + Double Half—Hitch

Difficulty
Easy

Warp
9 x 80cm

Finished piece
Approx. 18cm x 18cm plus fringe

STÉPHANIE'S TIPS

- Using the same rope and weaving techniques, you can create a set of table placemats to match this trivet, simply by scaling up the size.
- Play around with the warp length, finishing method and colour. It's the perfect small project to experiment with various techniques.

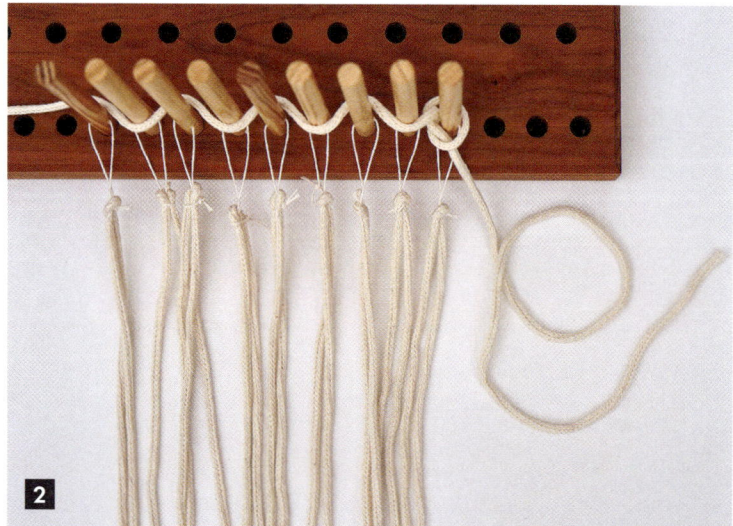

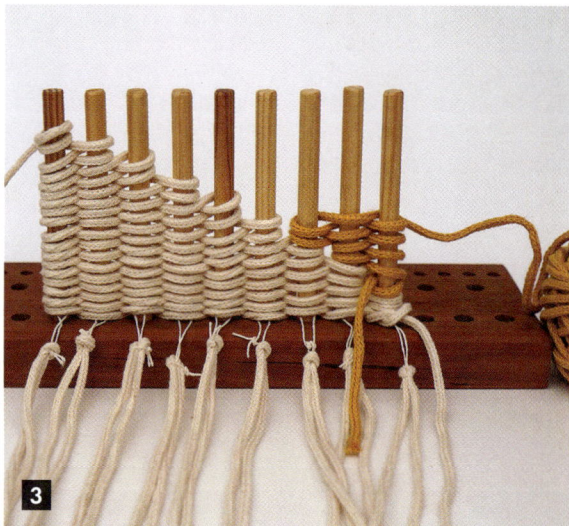

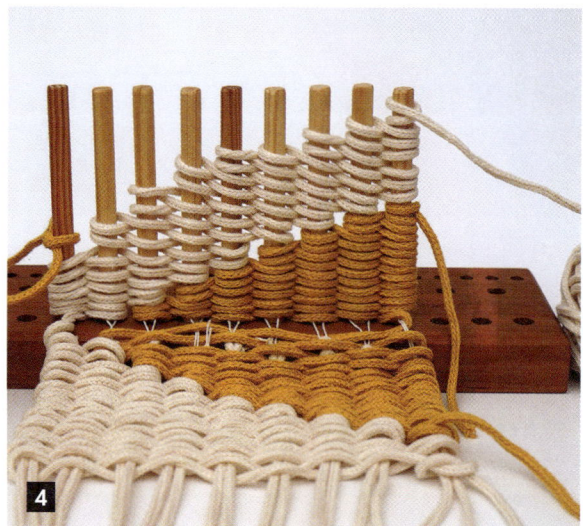

1. Thread 9 x 9mm pegs with a 10–15cm piece of string and tie in a knot to create your leashes. Cut 9 x 80cm lengths of the cotton cord, fold in half and secure to each leash using a lark's head knot.
2. Attach the cream rope to one of the outer pegs, leaving an end of approx 30cm (or the width of your piece plus 10cm). You will need this extra length to create the double half–hitch knot finishing technique when it is time to tie off.

3. Begin weaving with 2 rows across all 9 pegs, before dropping one peg every time you have woven 2 rows, as shown. Do not cut off the yarn, simply leave to one side. Attach the next colour and weave 2 rows on 1 peg, 2 rows on 2 pegs and so on until you have woven across 8 pegs. Push weaving down the warps.
4. To complete the first coloured triangle, begin reducing the rows, by weaving 2 rows on 7 pegs,

52

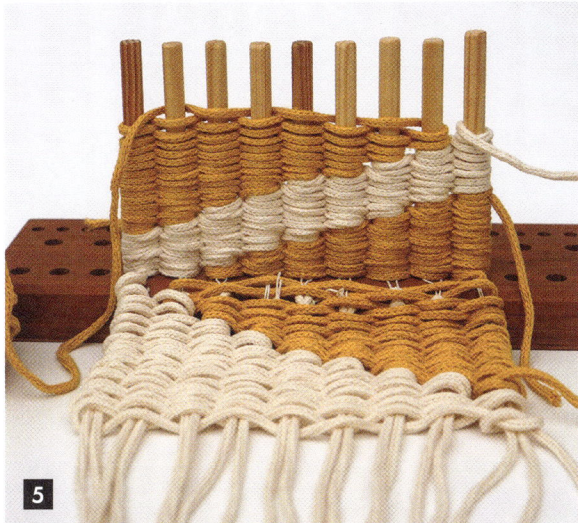

2 rows on 6 pegs and so on. Cut off the rope on the right side as shown. Take the cream rope and weave a diagonal line across the shape, make sure there are approx 5 rows on the outer left peg, as shown.

5. Fill in over the cream section with half a coloured triangle and push down, before completing the second triangle in both colours to finish the trivet.

6. Before cutting off the cream rope, as you did at the beginning of the piece, leave a 30cm tail to tie the double half hitch for this side of the trivet.

7. Lift the pegs off the loom and centre the piece so you have equal warp ends on both sides. Cut the rope free from the pegs and weave in the loose ends using a weaving needle or crochet/latch hook.

8. Using the long weft rope ends left on each side of the trivet, tie off each warp end twice around this lead rope, using the double half–hitch finishing technique. Cut the fringe to your preferred length and enjoy!

woven necklace

This stylish woven necklace is easily completed in an evening and oozes style. Change the size by using more weaving sticks, extending the tassel or the type of fibres. You may notice that I've double warped it. This provides weight to the necklace and allows this modern piece to sit perfectly for everyday use.

You will need

- 4 x 3mm weaving sticks
- Scheepjes Catona in Mustard, 4 ply — Approx. 20g
- Scheepjes Catona in Shell, 4 ply — Approx. 5g
- Weaving needle
- Scissors

Techniques
Plain weave + Shaping + Whipping Knot

Difficulty
Intermediate

Warp
8 x 1m

Finished piece
Approx. 3cm wide x 43cm long

STÉPHANIE'S TIP

- When weaving with a double warp on weaving sticks watch out for your tension as you work. If the weft is too taut, you may find it difficult to pull the sticks through.

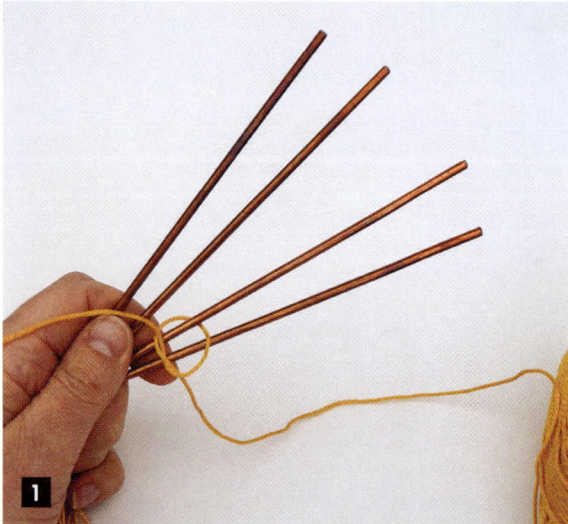

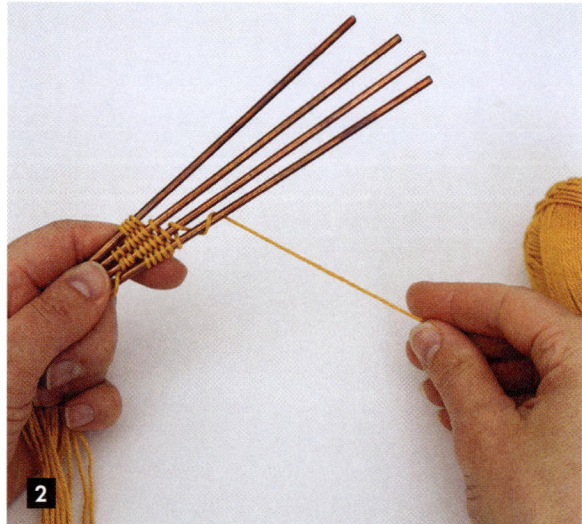

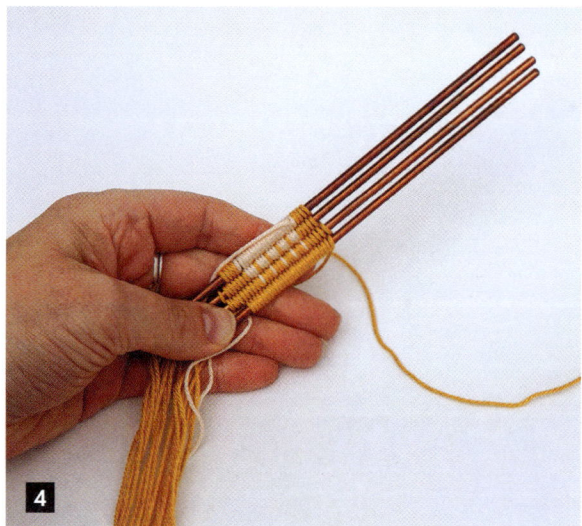

1. Cut 8 lengths of 1m of yarn so you have double lengths per weaving stick. Then attach the main colour (mustard) using an overhand knot, to one of the middle sticks.

2. Begin by weaving 3 rows on the 2nd and 3rd sticks, then weave 3 full rows on all the sticks, finishing by reducing by 1 peg, then 2 pegs and weaving one row on the right hand peg. Leave yarn to the side and do not cut it.

3. Securing the second colour (shell) to the left stick, begin by weaving one row on one stick, then one row on 2 sticks, then 3 sticks, 2 sticks and finally only 1 stick, as shown. Match the pattern with the mustard yarn.

4. Continue weaving the two colours simultaneously, following the pattern. Cut off the secondary colour. Then finish with 3–4 rows of your main colour. Do not cut the yarn.

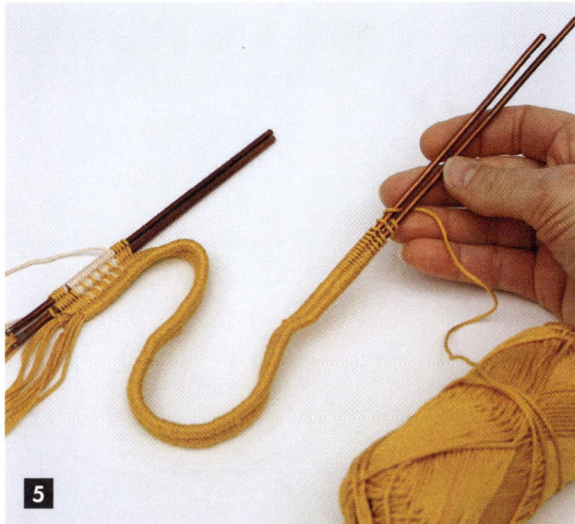

5. The next series of rows will be woven on only 2 sticks. Over and under, in a figure of eight, pulling the 2 weaving sticks upwards as the cord gets longer. Weave until you have a cord of approx. 35cm. Cut and tie off, using an overhand knot.

6. Attach the same main colour at the base and begin weaving on the remaining 2 sticks until the same length of woven cord as previously has been created. Cut and tie off.

7. With a double knot, tie each set of opposing warps together to form your necklace. Using a weaving needle, weave all the yarn ends and the top warps in their appropriate channel. Cut excess yarns.

8. Cut a yarn length of approx. 30cm of your chosen colour. Tie a whipping knot of approx. 2cm around the gathered bottom warp ends. Weave ends in and cut the tassel ends neatly.

bookish bookmark

I'm a bit of a bookworm and I always have a few novels on the go on my bedside table. These easy bookmarks will keep your place in style. Not only are they quick to create, but they are a great way to experiment with weaving techniques, patterns and colours. Weave it longer for a bracelet or camera strap.

You will need

- 5 x 3mm weaving sticks
- Scheepjes Catona in Mustard, 4 ply — Approx. 10g
- Scheepjes Catona in Blush, 4 ply — Approx. 10g
- Scheepjes Catona in Sage, 4 ply — Approx. 20g
- Weaving needle
- Scissors

Techniques
Plain Weaving + Shaping + Whipping knot

Difficulty
Easy

Warp
10 x 55cm

Finished piece
Approx. 3cm wide by 26cm long (with fringe)

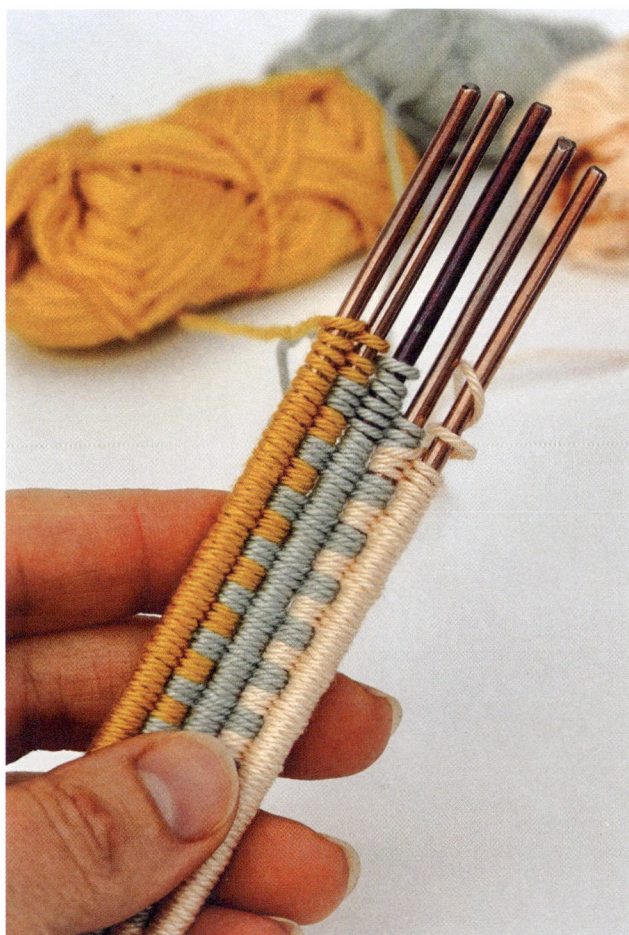

STÉPHANIE'S TIP

- You are doubling up the warps here to add rigidity to the bookmark. The warp colour will also create your end tassels so have fun choosing colours. I've finished with whipping knots, but feel free to braid the ends or use simple knots.

1. Begin by threading each of the 5 x 3mm weaving sticks with 2 warps of 55cm long. Attach the mustard yarn on the left hand stick, the blue on the next stick and the blush on the right hand stick, as shown.

2. Begin weaving all three colours simultaneously, by weaving 3 rows of each colour, following the pattern. Watch your tension and don't weave too tightly, as you may find it tricky to pull the sticks through.

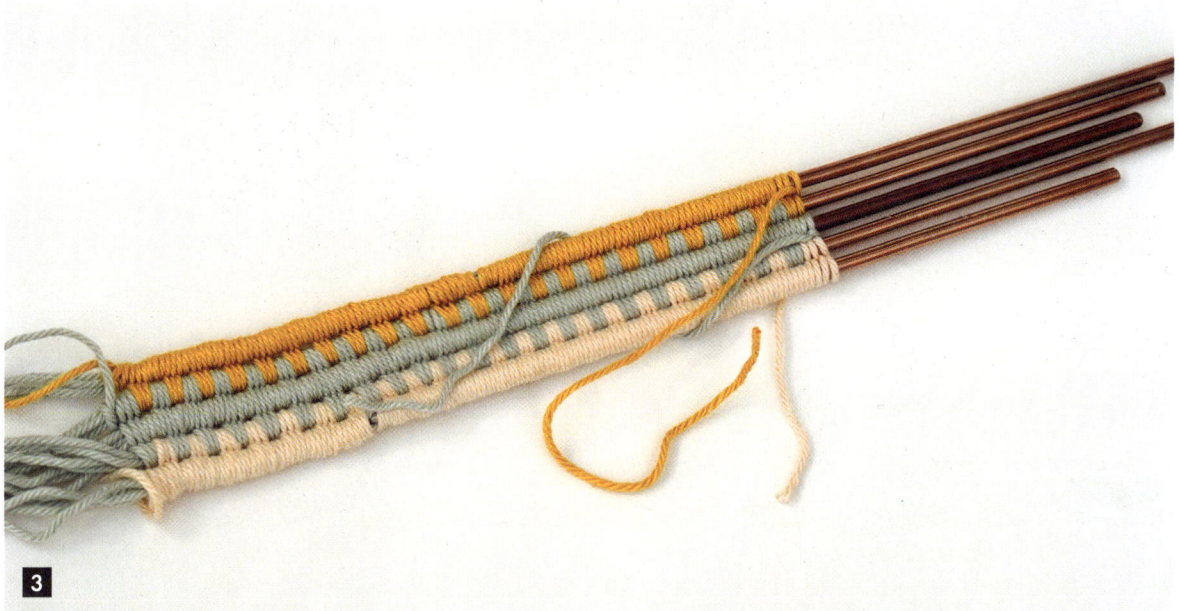

3. Weave for approx. 15cm. Pull each stick through the woven section, one by one, until you have equal warps lengths on both sides. Tidy up the loose ends, by weaving them back in using a weaving needle.

4. Separate your warp ends into 3 bundles of 7, 6 and 7 strands and tie each of them with a whipping knot using your colour of choice. Repeat on the other side.

round brooch

The statement brooch is making a comeback! There's no better way to jump on the trend than with a colourful piece of fibre design. It is perfect to get started with circular weaving as the pattern is woven all in one using copper weaving sticks. Play around with colours and lengths and make them for all your friends.

You will need

- 4 x 3mm weaving sticks
- Rico Ricorumi in Fox (orange) DK Yarn — Approx. 10g
- Rico Ricorumi in Lotus (coral) DK Yarn — Approx. 10g
- Rico Ricorumi in Lilac DK Yarn — Approx. 10g
- 32mm brooch pin
- Weaving needle
- Scissors

Techniques
Circular Weaving + Whipping Knot

Difficulty
Intermediate

Warp
4 x 50cm

Finished piece
Approx. 5cm diameter

1. Begin by threading 4 x 3mm weaving sticks with 50cm long warp threads each. Preferably choose the same colour as the main body of the piece to allow you to blend it easily when joining up the circle.

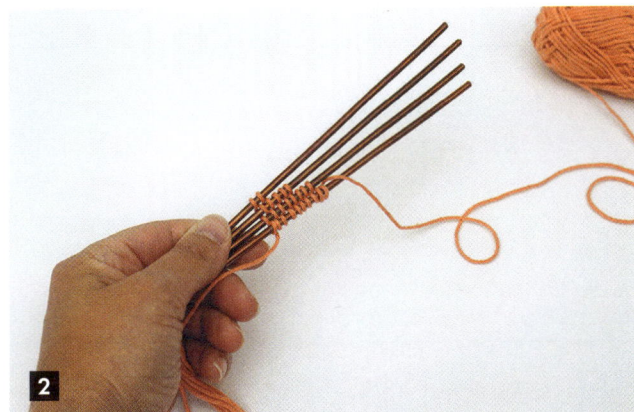

2. Using the same colour as the warp, tie the yarn end on the right peg. Weave 2 rows on all 4 pegs. Then 3 rows on 3 pegs, 3 rows on 2 pegs and 3 rows on the last peg.

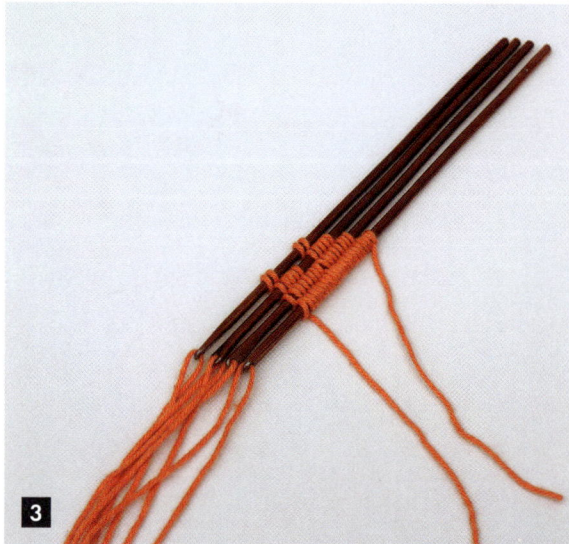

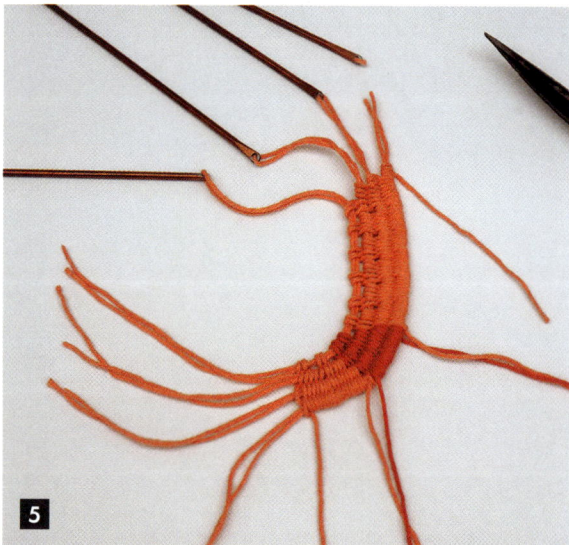

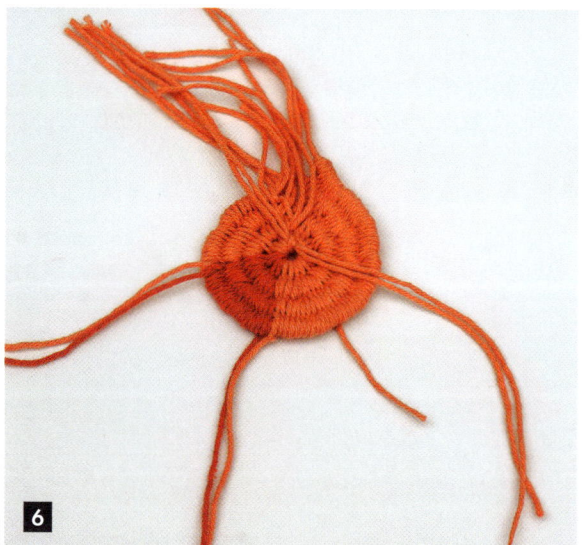

3. Repeat for a second triangle in the same colour, before cutting the yarn and tying off, leaving a 7–10cm tail.

4. Using your second colour and the same row pattern as above, weave 2 pie wedges before tying off the yarn. Returning to your original colour, weave 6 pies keeping a nice even tension throughout. You should be able to fit all of the 10 pie wedges on the

same sticks. Cut and tie off the yarn.

5. Starting with the left peg, pull it gently to bring the warp through the weft. This will be the centre of your circle. Then release the remaining sticks slowly, until the warps have travelled through the tunnels. Cut the sticks from the warp.

6. To complete your circle, begin pulling the 2 opposing centre warps tightly and tie off using

a double knot. Move on to the next warp pair, adjusting the circle and keeping the tension balanced, so that the circle remains flat.

7. Using a weaving needle, weave all of the loose yarn ends into their correct tunnel, approx. 1.5cm in. Cut off the excess near the base of the weave.

8. With your colour of choice, cut 10 equal lengths of approx. 20cm and, using a needle or crochet hook, insert through the centre of your woven circle.

9. Using a whipping knot in a contrasting colour, secure both fringe ends over the circle joins and cut equally for a neat finish.

10. Finally, sew or glue a 32mm brooch pin to the back of your piece. You are ready to showcase a little whimsical piece on your next outing!

chapter three: creative day camp

As a child, do you remember when Sundays were proper days off? When all the shops were closed and the streets were empty? Those Sundays would be the days to dig holes in the garden, read comic books under a blanket fort and try that new cookie recipe. I think it's time to reclaim that guiltless feeling of freedom by allowing yourself a day off to get crafty. Whether you're on your own, you've invited some friends over or want to get the kids involved, pick a project and spend your day off exploring creative freedom on the loom.

everyday garland

Of all the projects in this book, this everyday garland is by far the easiest to make for maximum impact. String your garland over a fireplace, above a bed, over your bookshelves or just hang on the wall. This is the perfect rainy day project for kids as you can use two straws if you don't have weaving sticks.

You will need

- Weaving sticks — 2 x 10mm (or straws or pegs)
- Women's Institute by Hobbycraft DK Yarn in Blush — Approx. 80g
- Chunky Debbie Bliss Paloma Yarn in Lilac — approx. 60g
- Chunky Debbie Bliss Paloma Yarn in Mint — Approx. 60g
- Stylecraft Chunky in Mustard — Approx. 60g
- Weaving needle
- Scissors

Techniques
Plain Weave + Whipping Knot

Difficulty
Easy

Warp
4 x 3m (shorter garland)
4 x 3.30m (middle garland)
4 x 3.60m (outer garland)

Finished piece
Approx. 120cm wide (hanging loosely)

STÉPHANIE'S TIPS
- These textured lengths of woven snakes can also be coiled into a rug, used as a curtain tie–back or even look pretty as contemporary wall art.

1. You will only need 2 weaving sticks, straws or pegs to create this versatile 3-tiered garland. Thread your sticks of choice with the length of warp you wish to start with. I've doubled the warp for these, as it helps with the rigidity of the garland. I have also added extra warp for the end tassels.

2. Starting with your first colour, tie a knot on one of the pegs and begin weaving in and out both pegs, in a figure 8. Cut off when you've reached the desired colour block length.

3. The woven yarn can be pushed down onto the warp to expose more of the weaving sticks. It does not need to be pushed completely off the sticks in order to continue weaving.

4. Once you have finished all three coils, tidy them up by weaving in all the loose ends using a weaving needle. Then take the 3 warp ends for one side and tie them together using a wrapping knot in a contrasting colour to create the tassels.

5. Repeat the whipping knot for the other side.

entry rug

Loosely inspired by Modernist master Piet Mondrian, I've used his simple rectangular shapes and fun modern colours to create this entry rug. Using cotton cord will make it solid yet soft underfoot. With rope available in all sorts of shapes and sizes, you are sure to find one to create this effortless multi−use rug.

You will need

- Peg loom of at least 50cm wide 25 x 9mm pegs
- Return of the Mac, 3mm Cord by Hobby Craft, in Ecru x 3. Any 3–4mm cotton rope will suit this project — Approx. 600g
- Return of the Mac, 3mm Cord by Hobby Craft in Terracotta x 1 — Approx. 120g
- Return of the Mac, 3mm Cord by Hobby Craft in Sage x 1 — Approx. 100g
- Return of the Mac, 3mm Cord by Hobby Craft in Mustard x 1 — Approx. 100g
- Weaving or tapestry needle or crochet/latch hook if using thicker rope
- Scissors

Techniques
Plain Weave + Whipping Knot + Leashes

Difficulty
Intermediate

Warp
25 x 3m

Finished piece
45cm wide x 60cm long

STÉPHANIE'S TIPS
- When creating a rug, ensure that the weave is quite tight when tying off the warps to keep everything in place whilst you are using it.

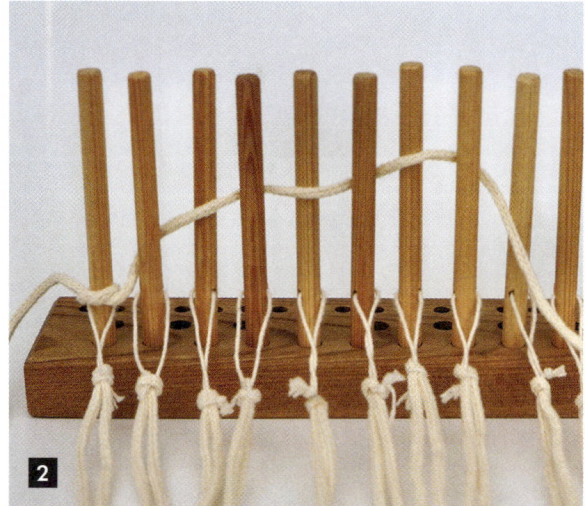

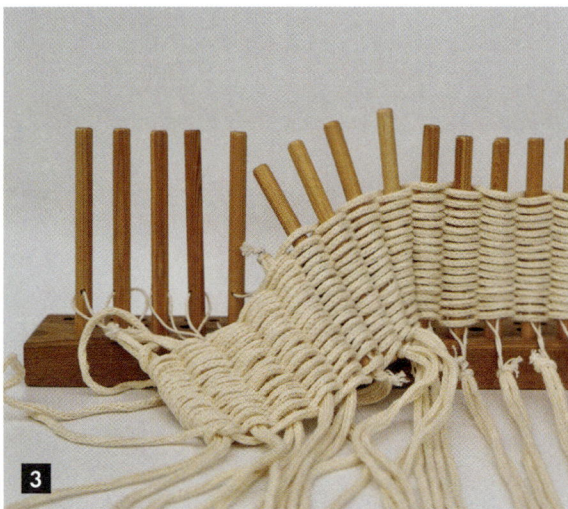

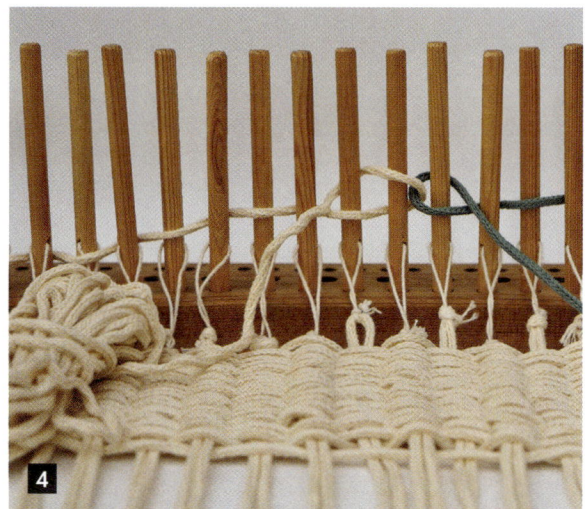

1. Begin by placing 25 x 9mm pegs in the slots of the peg loom. Thread each peg hole with a 10–15cm piece of string and tie in a knot to create your leashes. Then cut 25 x 2m lengths of the Ecru cord, fold in half and attach to each loop string using a lark's head knot. I've tied off the warp ends in groups of 3 or 4 to avoid the weft slipping off while weaving.

2. Attach the end of the Ecru cord to the left peg with a simple overhand knot. Begin weaving from left to right by passing the yarn in and out of the alternating pegs. At the end, turn around and weave back, from right to left in the opposite pattern to create the first row.

3. Continue to weave for approx. 7cm and leave the end of the cord on the far left peg. Remove the pegs, one by one, and slide the woven section down the warps.

4. Attach the end of the Sage cord on the right peg and start weaving alternating from the previous row. Stop roughly 9 pegs in. Using the Ecru cord, weave

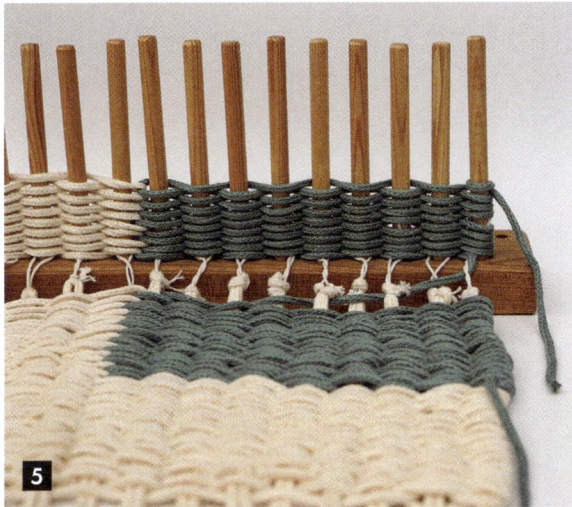

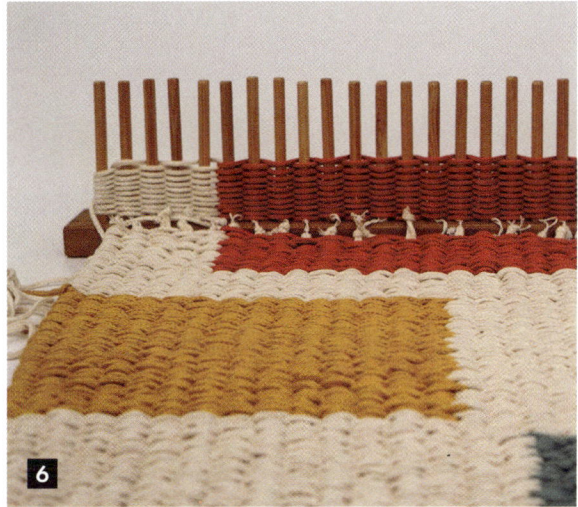

until you meet the Sage cord and both yarns are at the front of the loom in between the same two pegs.

5. To interlock the cords, cross the two cords in between the pegs, as shown, and continue the weaving pattern in the opposite direction. Continue weaving until you have a 10cm x 15cm rectangle.

6. Continue weaving and changing while following the pattern (or create your own!) whilst advancing the weft onto the warp each time you have woven ¾ up the pegs.

7. Once you have woven approx. 60cm, slide the completed panel down the warp using your fingers until warp ends are equal on both sides and tension has been distributed equally. Cut each warp to release it from the leashes. Using a tapestry needle weave in the loose cord ends and cut any excess.

8. Using 20 x 40cm lengths of Ecru cord, wrap each group of 5 warp ends using a whipping knot. Once you have wrapped all the warps on both sides, cut the tassels equally. Your rug is ready!

waves wall hanging

The sea has always inspired me. Using these dreamy blues, turquoises and mints bring me back to those warm balmy holidays by the coast. Using a chunky warp gives it a really lovely cushiness and the excess warp acts as fringe. I've used a wood dowel for my wall hanging, but driftwood or copper would work well too.

You will need

- Peg loom of at least 50cm wide 24 x pegs of 9mm
- Lion Brand Wool Ease in Cream — Approx. 180g
- Chunky Rico Designs in Teal — Approx. 100g
- Chunky Rico Designs Cotton in Dusty Blue — Approx. 50g
- Chunky World of Wool Chubbs in Mint — Approx. 50g
- Chunky World of Wool Chubbs in Sunset — Approx. 50g
- Chunky Debbie Bliss Paloma in Mint — Approx. 50g
- Wooden dowel of approx 20mm x 50cm
- Template (page 114)
- Weaving or tapestry needle
- Scissors

Techniques
Plain Weave + Curved Weave + Looped Warp + Leashes

Difficulty
Intermediate

Warp
24 x 1.50m

Finished piece
Approx. 45cm wide x 60cm long

1. Begin by threading 24 x 9mm pegs with a 10–15cm piece of string and tie in a knot to create your leashes. Using the looped warp method with the leashes will allow you to keep it in the all important loops to secure around the hanging dowel once the piece is completed.

2. Starting with the same colour yarn as the fringe, weave a 4–5 row plain weave section. This will help support the next step and prevent the rya knots from falling off. Leave the yarn end to one side and do not cut.

3. To create the first row of rya knots, cut 24 x 60cm yarn ends and secure 2 ends per pair of pegs to create each rya knot across the length of the pegs. Using the same colour yarn, left from the previous step, weave a few rows to lock it in. Again, do not cut the blue yarn as you will use it in the next step.

4. For the second row of rya knots, cut 22 x 60cm yarn ends and secure 11 pairs of rya knots on all the pegs except the two pegs on each end. Next, take the yarn, which you left aside, and wrap 2–3 times around the single end peg (with no rya) and start

weaving across. Stop at the last peg and wrap a few times to fill the gap on the left.

5. Keep going with the same colour and continue weaving until all the pegs are ¾ full. Then, one by one, lift the pegs and push the woven section onto the warp threads.

6. Weave a small section of the first colour and begin shaping, either by following the template or creating your own. Attach the second colour and follow the curves, filling the gaps until you are able to weave across all the pegs in a straight line. Push the

weaving down the warps.

7. Continue weaving until you have reached a length of approx. 35cm. To secure the loops needed to hang the dowel, thread a weaving needle with a 60cm length of the cream yarn (which should still be attached to the woven piece at this point). Weave over and under each of the single warped threads, as shown. Cut and tie off.

8. Next, release the yarn warp loops from their respective leashes. You can do this by either cutting the leash off or untying the lark's head knot by

pulling the peg through the leash.

9. To secure the wooden dowel, simply pass it through each warp loop. To tighten the loops, gently pull each pair from the bottom of the wall hanging.

10. Turn the piece over to expose the fringe and end warps. To secure everything in place, knot the warp ends using a half Damascus knot. Finally, hang the piece against a wall and cut the warps and the fringe to the desired shape!

planter basket

The versatility of this woven fibre vessel really makes this project a breeze. Whether you have an old plant pot that needs dressing up or want to use it to store yarns for your next project, it's up to you! These little planter baskets would look extra cute with added tassels around the border in toning colours.

You will need
- Peg loom of at least 30cm wide – 10 pegs of 9mm
- Chunky Debbie Bliss Paloma in Coral — Approx. 50g
- Chunky Debbie Bliss Paloma in Mint — Approx. 50g
- Chubbs Merino Wool in Rust — Approx. 50g
- Drops Andes in Cream — This twisted chunky yarn will be used as warp and weft — Approx. 120g
- Round wooden base of 200mm – The circumference of the wooden base will determine the length of finished woven textile.
- Weaving needle
- Scissors

Techniques
Hatching + Circular Weaving

Difficulty
Intermediate

Warp
10 x 160cm

Finished piece
64cm long (circumference) x 20cm wide (this will represent the height of the basket, this can vary according to preference)

STÉPHANIE'S TIP
- There are a wide selection of perforated wooden bases available on the market. This project could easily be adapted for a oval or square base.

1. Start by placing 10 x 9mm pegs into the holes of the peg loom. Thread each peg hole with a 10–15cm piece of string and tie in a knot to create your leashes. This allows the loom to accommodate a thicker wool warp. Then cut 10 lengths of 160cm of the cream warp yarn, fold in half and attach to each leash string using a lark's head knot.

2. To begin weaving using the irregular hatching technique, attach the cream yarn to the right peg and the first colour on the far left peg. Weaving each colour in a plain weave pattern until approximately midway on the loom, criss–cross each yarn between two pegs and weave back to their original position.

3. Continue weaving, alternating and changing where the two yarn colours meet. Once you have woven approximately ¾ of the pegs, lift each peg up, pull the warp through and replace each peg back in their original hole.

4. Weave while alternating colours on the left only whilst keeping the cream yarn on the right hand side.

Weave until you have reached a length of approx. 64cm then slide the textile piece down the warps and cut off the leashes.

5. With the piece off the loom, tidy up the loose yarn ends from the main textile by weaving the ends in. Leave the warp ends free, as you will be tying them together in the next step.

6. Using the wooden base as a guide, begin tying the adjoining warp pairs together. Loosely at first, until you are sure that you have the correct tension

throughout the cylinder shape and that the bottom fits slightly over the wooden base.

7. Remove the base and tighten the join knots with a double knot. Weave all the warp ends back into their appropriate 'tunnels'. Cut the excess yarn off.

8. With a weaving needle and a length of cream yarn, secure the base to the bottom of the cylinder using a whip stitch, ensuring that the knots are well hidden on the inside of the vessel.

round seat pad

This simple round seat cover is a very versatile design once you've masterered the technnique. As well as working well as a pad for a wooden chair seat, it can be refashioned into a round cushion cover, placemats or even a fun wall hanging by simply adding a few tassels for length.

You will need
- Peg loom of 30cm — 10 pegs of 9mm (or you can use graded pegs made specifically for weaving circles as shown)
- Drops Andes Chunky Yarn in Cream — Approx. 100g
- Super Chunky World of Wool Chubbs Yarn (Mustard + Peppermint + Lichen + Sky) — Approx. 50g each
- Chunky Debbie Bliss Paloma in Tangerine — Approx. 50g
- Anti–slip rubber underlay 40cm x 40cm — Large enough to cover your circle
- Thread and sewing needle
- Weaving needle
- Scissors

Techniques
Circular Weaving

Difficulty
Intermediate

Warp
10 x 256cm (longest warp)

Finished piece
The seat pad has a diameter of 35cm using the yarns in the project. The final diameter of your circle will vary depending on your chosen materials.

STÉPHANIE'S TIP
- If you are making a set of seat pads, you can follow my pattern and make them all match or adapt the design so each seat pad is slightly different.

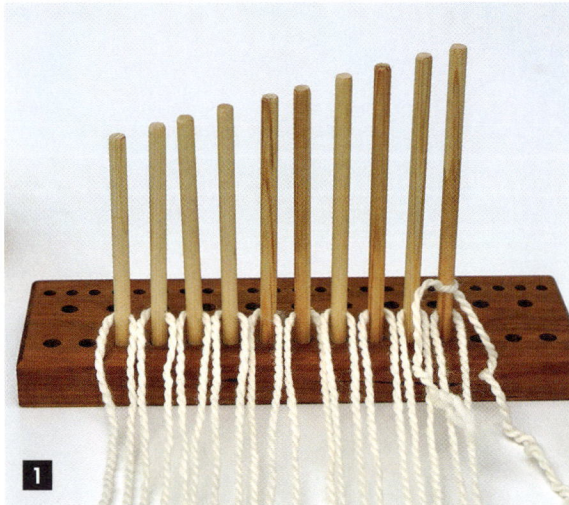

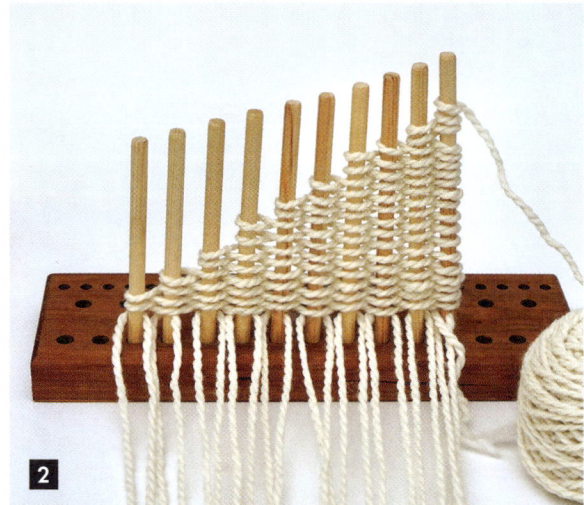

1. Cut 10 lengths of 256cm of your chosen yarn warp. Preferably use a colour that can easily be hidden between two pie segments of the same colour (cream in this case). Fold it in half and thread through the hole of each peg using a threader or needle. You can reduce the length of the warps slightly as you warp towards the centre of the circle.

2. Beginning with the same colour as the warp, attach the yarn to what will be the outside of the circle, in this case the right hand peg. Weave a triangle by weaving 2 rows on all the pegs, before reducing by one peg. Finish with wrapping the right hand peg twice.

3. Continue creating the coloured triangles, pushing down the yarns every one or 2 sections, depending on the sticks used. To follow the exact pattern pictured; Weave 3 cream sections, 2 orange, 1 red, 3 cream, 1 mint, 2 light blue, 4 cream, 2 green and finish with 2 cream sections. For a total of approx. 20 pie segments.

4. While pushing the weft down onto the warp, try and keep the centre warps pulled slightly. This will help you work out how many triangles you will need to make in order to create a complete circle.

5. If you are happy with the density and shape of the circle, remove the pegs from the loom and cut them free. Reshape the circle using the warps, finishing with equal warp ends on both sides.

6. Tie each warp with their adjoining pair, using a double knot. Keep an eye on the tension in order to create a flat circle.

7. Using a large eyelet weaving needle, tidy up the loose ends by weaving in the warps in their own tunnels and any other yarn ends found around the piece. Cut excess yarn.

8. To finish the seat cover and ensure it stays in place, cut a round piece of anti–slip rubber underlay approx. 1 cm smaller than the woven circle. I found it easier to sew a small stitch to secure it in the centre and then sew it around the circle, using a whip stitch.

crossover cowl

This crossover cowl will soon become a cosy winter staple due to it's chunky and soft wool. Using a knit–like combination of soumak and reverse soumak textured stitches gives it extra squishiness. Make it a little longer and finish the ends with tassels or a Damascus edge to transform it into a scarf.

You will need

- Peg loom of at least 30cm wide – 15 pegs of 9mm
- Super Chunky Crazy Sexy Wool by Wool and the Gang in Cream – 400g
- Chunky Chubbs by World of Wool in Mustard – Approx. 25g
- Drops Andes in Cream — This twisted chunky yarn will be used as warp – Approx. 50g
- Weaving needle
- Scissors

Techniques
Soumak + Reverse Soumak + Leashes

Difficulty
Easy

Warp
15 x 220cm

Finished piece
26cm wide x 80cm long

1. Thread 15 x 9mm pegs with a 10–15cm piece of string and tie in a knot to create your leashes. This will allow the loom to accommodate a thicker wool warp. Then attach warp yarns to the leashes using lark's head knots.

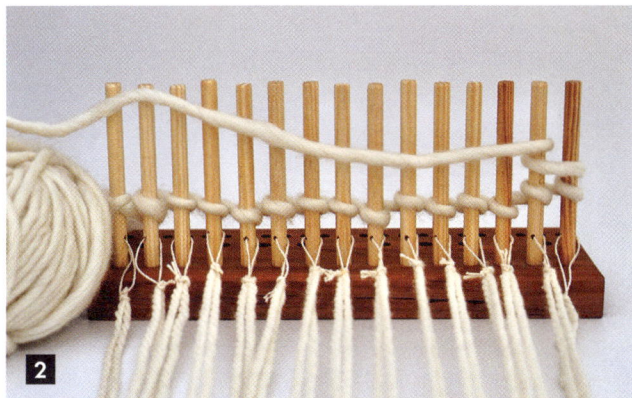

2. Secure the end of the cream yarn with an overhand knot and weave the first pass across all the pegs using the reverse soumak stitch, from left to right. Do not pull the yarn too much but keep an even tension throughout the piece.

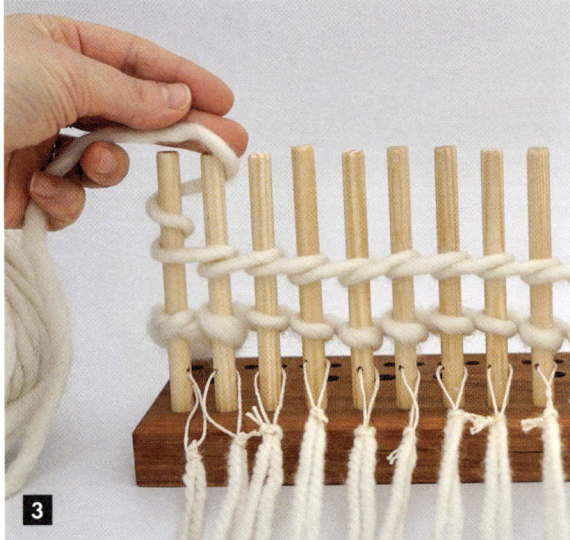

3. Once you have reached the end, wrap the yarn around the last peg and continue weaving using the soumak stitch, from right to left.

4. Keep on weaving with a combination of one pass soumak and one pass of reverse soumak until you have woven approx. 50cm then cut the yarn end and tie off.

5. Using the same two weaving techniques, weave

a 6–7cm section using the mustard yarn. Cut and tie it off.

6. Finish weaving the last cream section in soumak and reverse soumak, until you have reached a length between 80cm and 90cm. Bring the woven textile down the warp using your fingers, until you have equal warp ends on both sides. Cut off the pegs.

7. Before creating our twist to bring the cowl ends

together, I would recommend tidying up all the loose ends of yarn on the main panel by weaving in the loose ends.

8. Laying the fabric flat, take the top right corner and while twisting, bring it down to the bottom left corner. Next, bring the bottom right corner to the top left corner. That should give you a twist in the fabric.

9. At first, loosely tie off each opposing pair of warps, using a double knot. I would recommend trying the cowl on for size, adjusting it and then securing together the knots, closing together the twisted circular piece.

10. Using a weaving needle with a large eyelet, weave in the warp ends through 3 or 4 rows, keeping each warp into its own 'tunnel'. Now bring on the cold weather!

chapter four: weekend craftcation

Life is busy and weekends for many of us can be a welcome opportunity to get away from the desk to re–centre, relax and take time for ourselves. I love to lose myself in a project, as it helps with building self—esteem and gives me an instant mood lift. These projects will give you the perfect combination of creativity and self–care with a stylish room refresh with the skyline cushion or the ambitious (and very cool) desert bed headboard.

skyline cushion

If you want to give a room a quick facelift, a few colourful cushions will do the trick. These were the first ever creations that I made using the peg loom. I loved the pop of texture they instantly brought to our mustard velvet sofa. This playful version lets you practice mixing soumak and plain weave with a chunky yarn.

You will need

- Peg loom of at least 40cm wide — 19 pegs of 9mm
- Super Chunky Wool Ease in Fisherman by Lion Brand — Approx. 200g
- Chunky Chubbs Merino Wool in Rust — Approx. 80g
- Super Chunky Chubbs Merino Wool in Peppermint — Approx. 80g
- Super Chunky MillaMia in Sunshine — Approx. 80g
- Super Chunky MillaMia in Seagull — Approx. 80g
- Hobbycraft Women's Institute Soft & Chunky in Cream. This strong cushy yarn will be used as warp — Approx. 50g
- Cushion insert 32cm x 52cm
- Fabric backing — 2 pieces of 34cm x 40cm
- Tapestry needle
- Sewing machine or needle and thread
- Scissors

Techniques
Leashes + Plain Weave + Soumak + Interlocked Weft

Difficulty
Intermediate

Warp
19 x 1.60m

STÉPHANIE'S TIP
- This cushion is designed to fit a standard 32cm x 52cm pillow insert, easily found on the high street or online. The finished woven cushion will measure 54cm x 34cm.

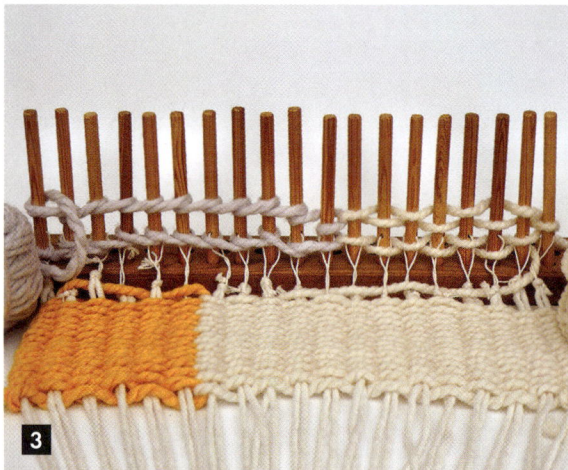

1. Cut 19 x 1.60 m of chunky cream yarn, fold in half and attach to each leash string using a lark's head knot. The width of the pegs should equal approx. 34cm. Begin by securing the cream yarn on the right hand peg and the mustard yarn to the left hand peg. Weave the mustard yarn over 6 pegs then pick up the cream yarn and weave until you meet the mustard yarn. Using the interlocking technique, criss—cross the yarn in between the two pegs and continue weaving in the opposite direction.

2. Once you have woven approx. ¾ of the pegs and both colours have returned to their side of the loom,

cut and tie off the mustard only, as the cream yarn will be used continuously throughout the piece. Slide woven sections onto the warps.

3. For the lilac section, I've used the soumak stitch interlocked with the cream yarn. As you need to wrap twice around the 'turnaround' peg, ensure that the cream yarn has interlocked the first row, returned to the right hand side, back towards the middle and interlocked the second 'row' before before weaving both yarns in opposite directions.

4. Following the image or your own design, continue weaving alternating colours with plain weave and

96

soumak stitches, always keeping the cream yarn on the right hand side. Weave until the length reaches approx. 54cm then slide the panel down the warps until you have equal lengths on both sides and adjust the tension of the sections.

5. Clean up the panel by weaving in all the loose yarn ends using a tapestry needle. Tie off warp ends in groups of three, with an overhand knot on both sides of the woven panel. On one end, you will be left with 5 warps that can be tied off in one group of 3 warps and one pair, as shown.

6. To create the envelope backing, cut two pieces of fabric 34cm x 40cm. Then fold one of the 34cm edges twice by 1cm and pin, as shown. Repeat with the other piece. Sew in place, close to the folded edge.

7. Place the woven panel and the two backing fabric pieces with the right sides together, lining up the edges. Ensure the two fabric pieces with sewn edges overlap in the centre. Pin in place and sew around the rectangle with a 1cm seam allowance.

8. Turn the sewn envelope inside out ready to insert the cushion pad. Fluff it up and place in your favourite spot to admire your work!

bolster cushion

This is a project to really sink your teeth into as it uses multiple techniques to bring it all together. I love the versatility of a bolster cushion and the dimension it brings to a space. I can see this cushion also being used as a yoga bolster, used in restorative poses to support different parts of the body.

You will need
- Peg loom of at least 50cm wide
- Super Chunky Wool Ease by Lion Brand in Fisherman — Approx. 200g
- Chunky Chubbs Merino Wool in Rust — Approx. 80g
- Chunky Debbie Bliss Paloma in Tangerine — Approx. 80g
- Super Chunky MillaMia in Yellow — Approx. 50g
- Chunky So Cool + So Soft Cotton by Rico in Blush — Approx. 50g
- Hobbycraft WI Soft & Chunky in Cream. Also used as warp — Approx. 80g
- Bolster insert — 41cm x 16cm
- Template (page 98)
- Weaving needle
- Needle and thread
- Scissors

Techniques
Plain Weave + Shaping + Interlocking + Circular Weaving

Difficulty
Experienced

Warp
23 x 140cm (main piece) + 8 x 120cm (2 circular ends)

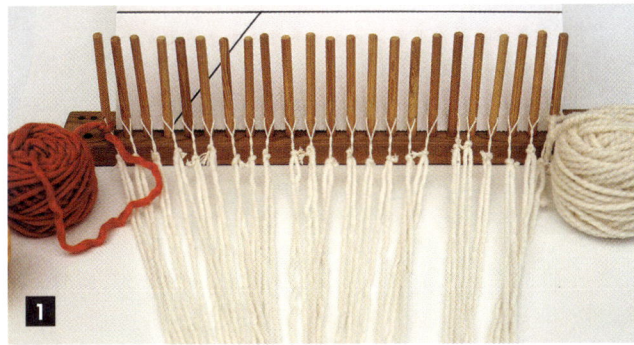

1. Thread each peg hole with a 10–15cm piece of string and tie in a knot to create your leashes. Cut 23 x 140 cm of chunky cream yarn, fold in half and attach to each leash string using a lark's head knot. For this piece I found it useful to follow a paper template placed behind the piece.

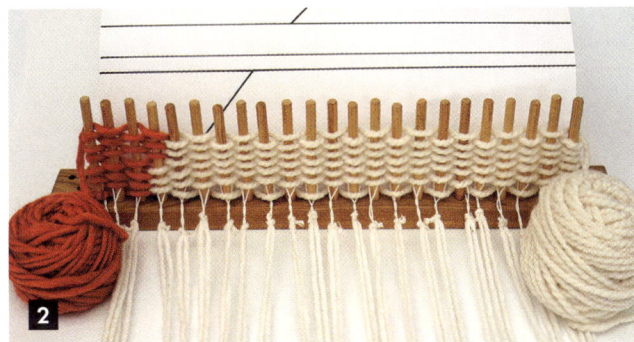

2. Begin by securing the cream yarn to the right and the rust yarn to the left using a simple overhand knot. To achieve the stepper angle in the pattern, I've woven 3 rows of each colour on each peg, before reducing it by one peg after the 3 rows. Interlock the yarns between the pegs, as shown, to avoid any gaps in the textile.

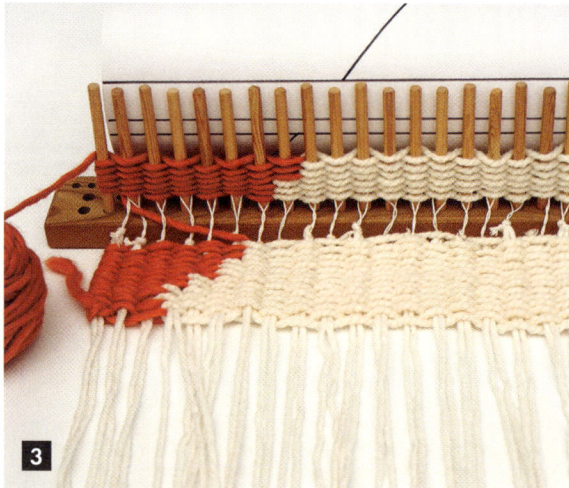

3. Once you have reached ¾ of the pegs and the yarns are back to their initial starting point, push the section down onto the warps. Keep them quite close to the pegs, as you will continue weaving with the same yarns to finish that specific colour section.

4. Continue weaving and changing colours following the template (or your own!) until you have reached a length of approx. 53cm. Push the piece down the warps until you have equal warp ends on both sides. Keep the tension nice and even throughout, to give some breathing space to your textile.

5. Cut the main panel off the leashes. Then tidy up the piece by weaving in all the ends using a large eyelet needle (not the warps!). Cut excess yarn off. The finished piece will be approximately 53cm high x 43cm wide.

6. Using the bolster insert to guide you, begin by tying off the first pair of end warps with a double knot (gently, as it may need adjustment after) and working your way through all the pairs. Ensure that the 2 end warps are equally pulled and tied together to approx. 16cm diameter circle.

7. Tidy up all the loose ends by weaving them in approx. 5-7cm down into their 'tunnels'. Cut excess yarn ends and adjust your woven textile to hide the join neatly.

8. To create the two end circles, attach new warps lengths to 4 x 9mm pegs. I've used the same length of 120cm for all 4 pegs to create our 16cm diameter circle. Begin weaving the first pie segment with 2 rows on the inner peg, which will be the middle of your circle, followed by 2 rows on each of the remaining 3 pegs. Repeat for 11 pie segments.

9. Push the wedges down the warps and begin pulling and tying off the adjoining warps, starting with the middle of the circle and working your way outward. Clean up the yarn ends by weaving them in their respective 'tunnels'. Cut off excess ends and repeat for a second circle.

10. Now it's time to assemble all your pieces and complete the project. Whilst keeping the bolster insert inside the circular cover, secure both circles using a needle and thread in a figure 8 stitch, catching both outer warps from the circle and the main piece.

bench cover

There's something very comforting about a wooden bench, isn't there? It has a heritage farmhouse vibe that emulates comfort, closeness and family unity. Whether your bench is used in the dining room, as a coffee table or in your hallway, this woollen cover will keep the atmosphere (and bottoms) cosy.

You will need
- Peg loom of at least 30cm wide – 11 pegs of 9mm
- Dreadlock wool (roving that has been washed and rolled) – approx. 600g
- Chunky MillaMia Super Soft Merino Wool in Eau de Nil & Sunshine – Approx. 40g each
- Super Chunky 100% Homestead Yarn by Stitch and Story in Pink Peony — Approx. 40g
- Rug Warp in Cream (to match the dreadlock wool for a seamless look) — Approx. 50g
- Anti–slip rubber underlay 120cm x 25cm
- Sewing needle and thread
- Crochet hook or latch hook
- Scissors

Techniques
Twining + Basket Weave + Plain Weave + Leashes

Difficulty
Intermediate

Warp
11 x 3.20m

Finished piece
Approx. 26cm wide x 120cm long

STÉPHANIE'S TIP
- The yarn lengths to create the design above (yarns folded in half to create the basket weave) are green = 14.5m; wool = 3m; mustard = 7m; wool = 4.4m; pink = 12.8m

1. Using the 25mm spaced pegs, attach leashes to each peg in order to accommodate the wool rug warp. Then using a lark's head knot, secure each warp to the leashes. To create a small heading, twine 3 rows of the same wool yarn as the warp to secure the basket weave.

2. Cut approx. 40 metres of the dreadlock wool and fold it in half. Using the middle loop, wrap it around one of the outer pegs and begin weaving the doubled up yarn in a basket weave, ensuring the two yarns remain stacked neatly one on top of each other. The dreadlock wool will need to be pulled a little tighter than usual, as it tends to expand when taken off the pegs.

3. The doubled—up length of wool should give approx. 36cm of woven textile before you need to tie off the ends with a simple half—loop on the outer peg. Leave approx. 10—15cm of yarn tails, which will be woven in at the end.

4. Using 3 coloured yarns (preferably the thickest yarns you can find!) weave colour blocks of varying sizes (see Stephanie's Tip for exact lengths), alternating

between coloured yarn and a few rows of dreadlock wool. Use the same basket weave method throughout.

5. Using the remainder of the 600g dreadlock wool length, fold it in half and weave approx. 60 cm of basket weave until you have reached a total 120cm (or longer if you have a longer bench!).

6. Finish with 3 rows of twining with rug warp (as you did in step 2) in order to lock in the thicker yarn. Slide the woven textile down the warp until you have equal warp ends on each side of your piece and cut off the pegs.

7. Finish the warp edging using the Damascus finishing technique, and weave in the warp and yarn ends, on what will be the reverse side of the bench cover. As the dreadlock yarn is quite thick, using a latch hook or crochet hook will help tucking these ends in smoothly.

8. Cut a piece of anti-slip underlay slightly smaller than your piece and sew it by hand using a whip stitch, as shown, to the underside of the cover. This will help keep your new cosy cover securely in place on the bench.

modern clutch

The clutch is having a moment just now as the perfect arm candy to brighten up your next summer outfit. I love the flexi–frame that makes it easy to open and keeps items securely in place! Why not use this versatile bag as a travel bag to hold all your essentials for your next night away?

You will need

- Peg loom of at least 30cm wide – 4mm pegs
- Chunky So Cool + So Soft Cotton by Rico in Blush — Approx. 60g
- Chunky So Cool + So Soft Cotton by Rico in Rust — Approx. 80g
- Chunky So Cool + So Soft Cotton by Rico in Cream — Approx. 100g
- Chunky Andes by Drops in Lilac — Approx. 60g
- Cotton DK string for the warp — Approx. 50g
- 30cm Flex Frame by Prym
- Fabric of your choice for the lining — 34cm x 64cm
- Template (page 106)
- Sewing machine
- Weaving needle
- Scissors

Techniques
Plain weave + Shaping + Whipping Knot

Difficulty
Experienced

Warp
23cm x 1.5m

Finished piece
30cm wide x 42cm long (folded in half)

STÉPHANIE'S TIPS

- For this particular piece, I drew an A3 paper template to use during the weaving process. It was easy to keep track of each coloured section and their sizes. When using a template, the woven section will begin at the bottom of the paper. You may need to fold the template to see the design against the pegs.

- Choose a thinner fabric for the lining as it will make the sewing process easier using a sewing machine. The project can also simply be sewn by hand using a sturdy needle.

1. Begin by placing 23 x 4mm pegs on the peg loom, these should equate to 30cm wide. Cut 23 lengths of 1.50m of warp, fold in half and thread through each peg. If you are using quite a thin warp string, you can tie them together on the bottom to prevent the warp from tangling in the early stages.

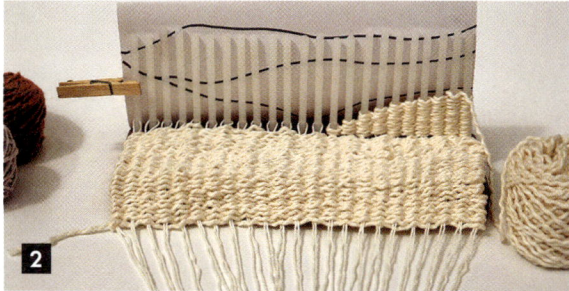

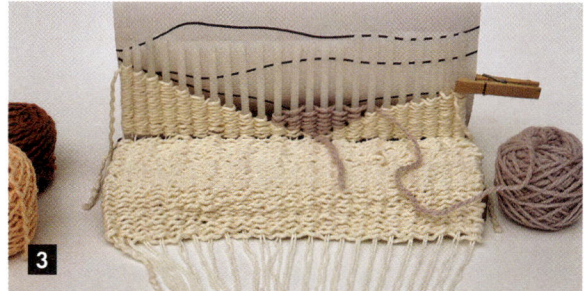

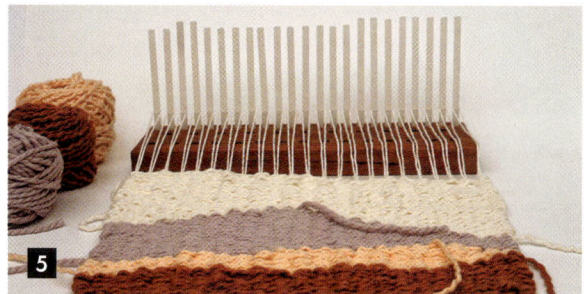

2. Secure the yarn with an overhand knot and plain weave approx. 10cm before pushing it down the warp, keeping the fabric close to the pegs. Continue weaving the cream yarn in the curved pattern, as shown on the template.

3. Once the cream section is done, weave the lilac section by starting in the centre and plain weave, following the lines. Stop when you have woven the desired shape and tie off.

4. Attach the next colour and weave until the yarn has travelled across all the pegs creating a straight line. This is the perfect chance to push the woven sections down onto the warps.

5. Continue filling in the shapes using the template, mirroring both halves with the same colours. This will ensure the pattern is similar on both sides of the clutch.

6. Once you have reached a length of approx. 42cm of textile, push the woven section down the warp strands. Ensure there are equal lengths of warp on both sides. Cut from the pegs.

7. When you are happy with the density and position of the weave, tie off warps on one end of the fabric using a Damascus knot. Repeat for the other side.

8. Time to weave all the loose warps and weft ends into the fabric using a large eyelet tapestry needle. Snip off excess yarn.

9. Place the lining fabric over the woven piece, iron and pin in place while folding in approx. 1.5cm around the edges of your piece. Machine sew in place with a 1cm hem. Place the fabric underneath the woven piece so the feed dogs to do their work and move the fabric smoothly as you sew. You may need to adjust the pressure foot to accommodate the thickness of the piece. You could also hand sew it with a whip stitch or a back stitch.

10. Fold each short end approx. 4cm and sew across with a 1cm hem. It can be hard to advance the fabric in the sewing machine, as both sides are woven. You may need to pull the fabric through or sew by hand.

Following the instructions for your chosen flex frame, insert it in the open folds and secure in place.

11. Stitch the pouch closed by hand using the cream yarn and a whipstitch (sewing around both sides with cream yarn). Using a large eyelet needle, create a secure binding edge over both sides by having each loop as close together as possible. Use pliers if the needle gets stuck!

12. To create the tassels, cut approx. 20 lengths of yarn and tie a 30cm length around the middle of the bundle using a double knot. With a contrasting colour, tie a whipping knot 3cm from the top. Attach your tassels to the flex frame and enjoy!

desert headboard

This statement piece radiates cool desert vibes with its soft curves, gentle hues and natural wood. It was created to sit behind a double bed, but can easily be adapted to suit your own space. The braided cord gives a modern feel, but it would look great using merino roving, dreadlock wool or any other twisted rope.

You will need

- 42 x 22mm round wooden dowels. The ones used here are 100cm poplar dowels
- Bobiny 9mm Jumbo Braided Cotton Rope in Wild Raspberry 1kg, Blush 500g, Mustard 600g, Cream 1kg
- Template (page 110)
- Needle and thread or strong glue

Techniques
Plain Weave + Shaping

Difficulty
Experienced

Warp
No need, as the dowels act as warp

Finished piece
140cm wide x 100cm high

STÉPHANIE'S TIP

- Once the piece is completed, it may help to use a hammer to bang the dowels down to they sit neatly in a straight line. If needed, a dab of super–strength glue to the bottom row will prevent the cord from slipping.

1. To gently ease into this gigantic project, you'll firstly need to take over a large table, bed or floor space to lay all your dowels nicely side by side. You can use the line template on page 117 to guide you for this design.

2. Begin by attaching the bottom colour (in this case the darkest cord) using an overhand knot. Weave, over and under each dowel for 4–5 rows while ensuring that you adjust the tension accordingly, so that the dowels lay flat.

3. Continue weaving the yarn, whilst pushing it upwards for approx. 20cm before beginning to reduce the number of woven dowels to form the first curved shape from the pattern. Attach the second 'wave' of colour to the left dowel and bring it back to the centre to fill in the first colour's lower curve.

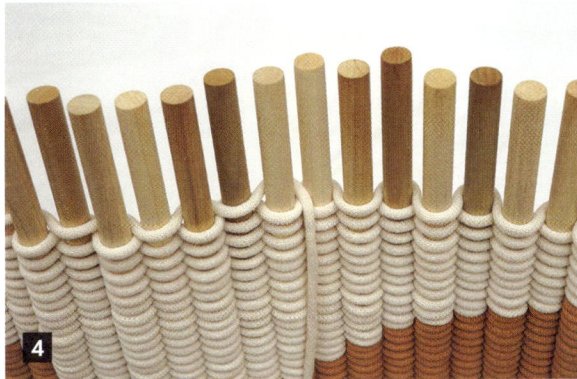

Continue weaving until you have the desired curve.

4. Weave in the last two coloured cords to create the rest of the pattern, while continuing to pull the dowels through and pushing the woven cord in place. Once you have ¾ of the dowels filled, you can prop all of them upright on the floor and continue to weave like you would a regular peg loom.

5. Using the thick cord may prove tricky to hide all the loose yarn ends by weaving them in. Instead, you can either use a dab of fabric glue or a needle and thread to sew in the loose ends for a seamless finish on the back of your piece.

6. Depending on how high your bed or mattress is, you can either install the headboard by resting it against the wall or secure it using U–shaped brackets or a few wall screws hidden under a loop.

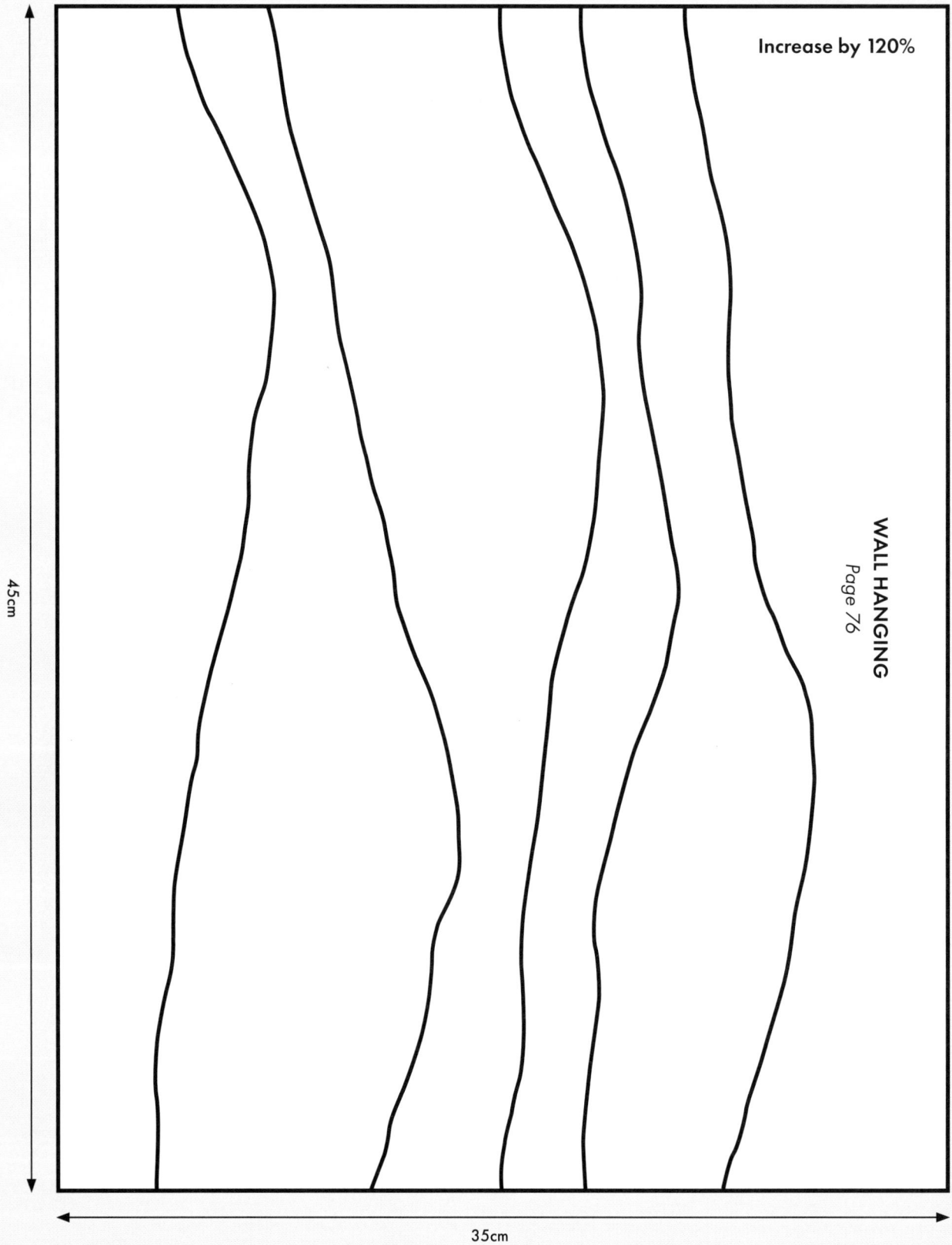

Increase by 120%

45cm

35cm

WALL HANGING
Page 76

Increase by 212%

53cm

43cm

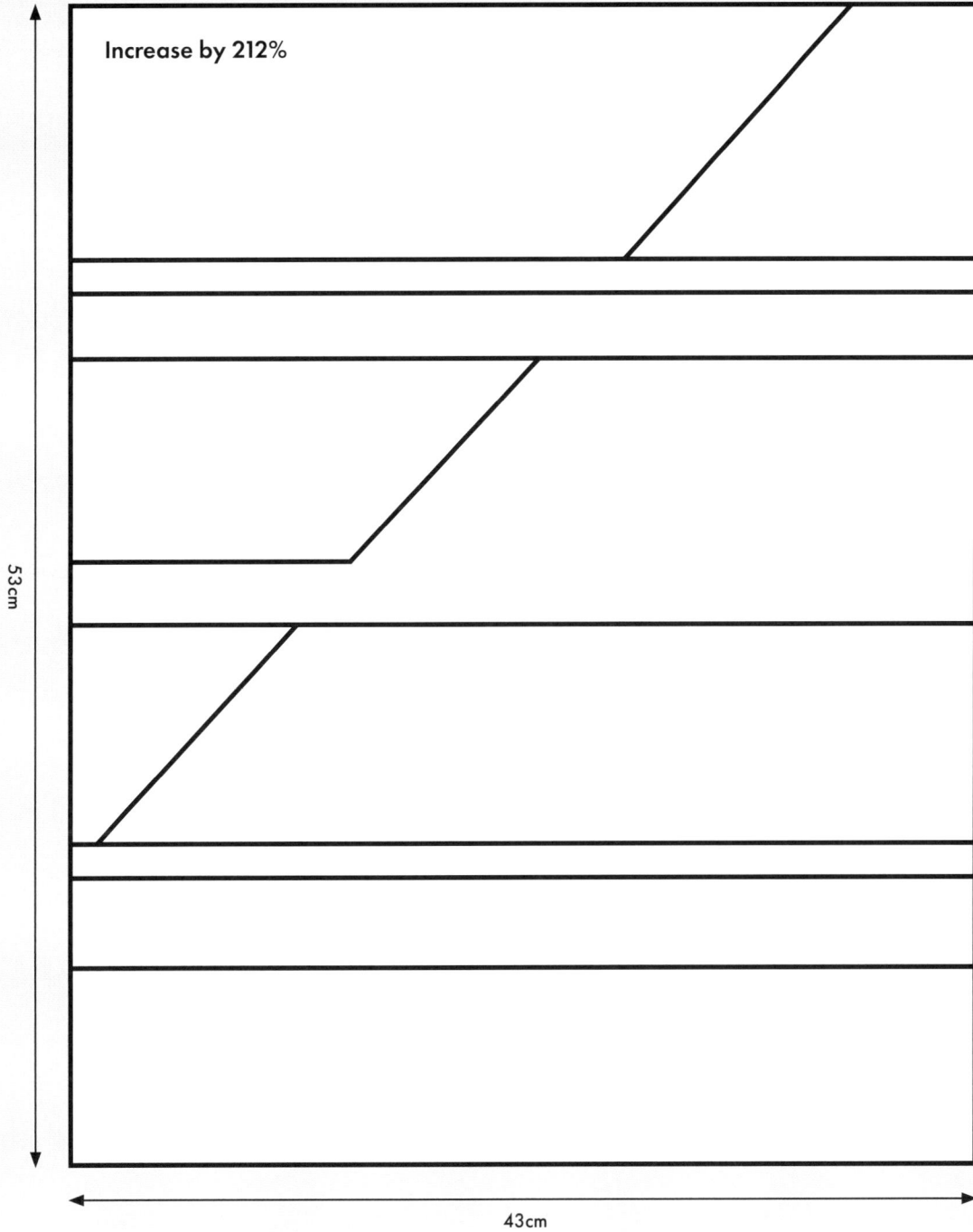

BOLSTER
Page 98

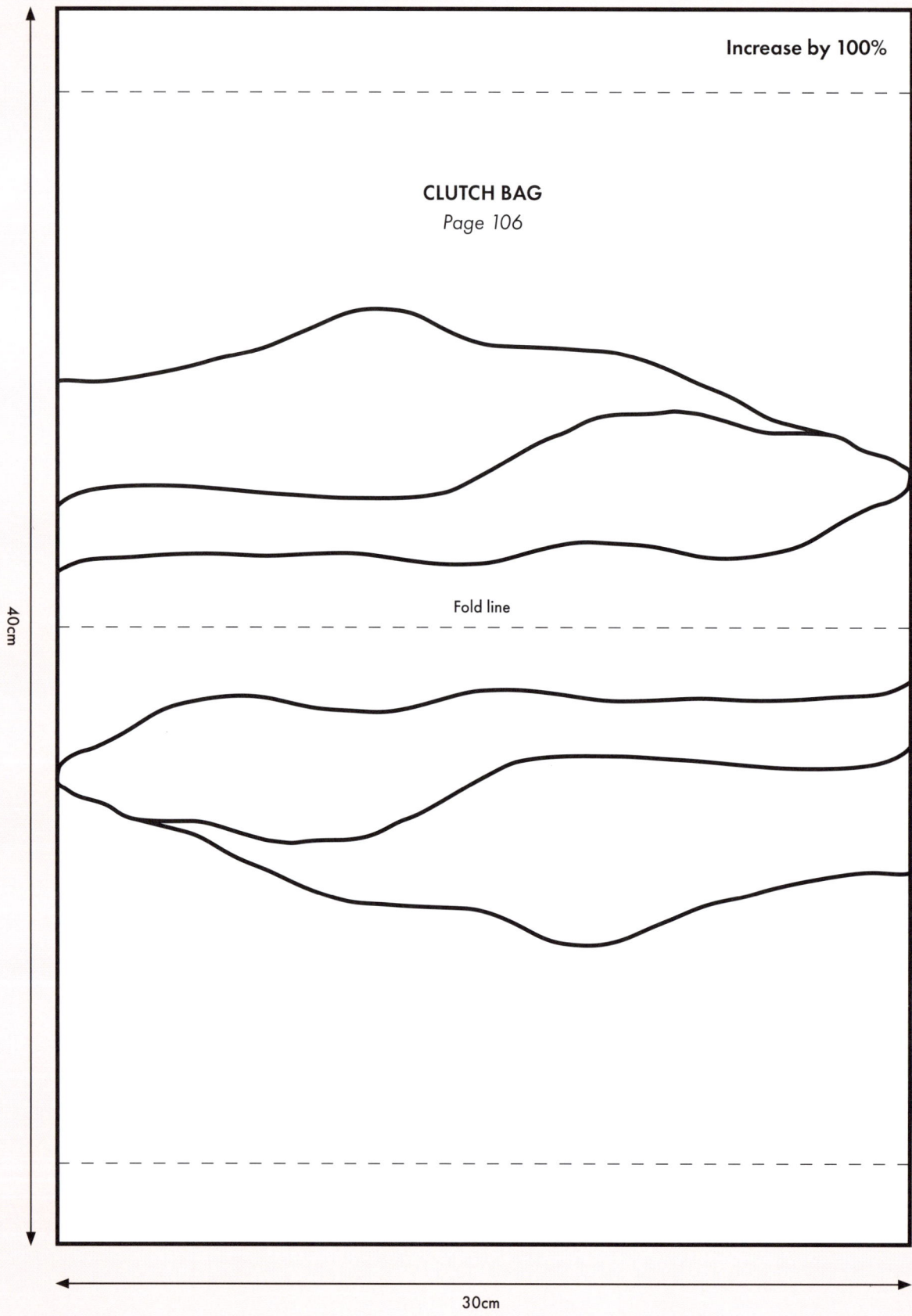

Increase by 100%

CLUTCH BAG
Page 106

Fold line

40cm

30cm

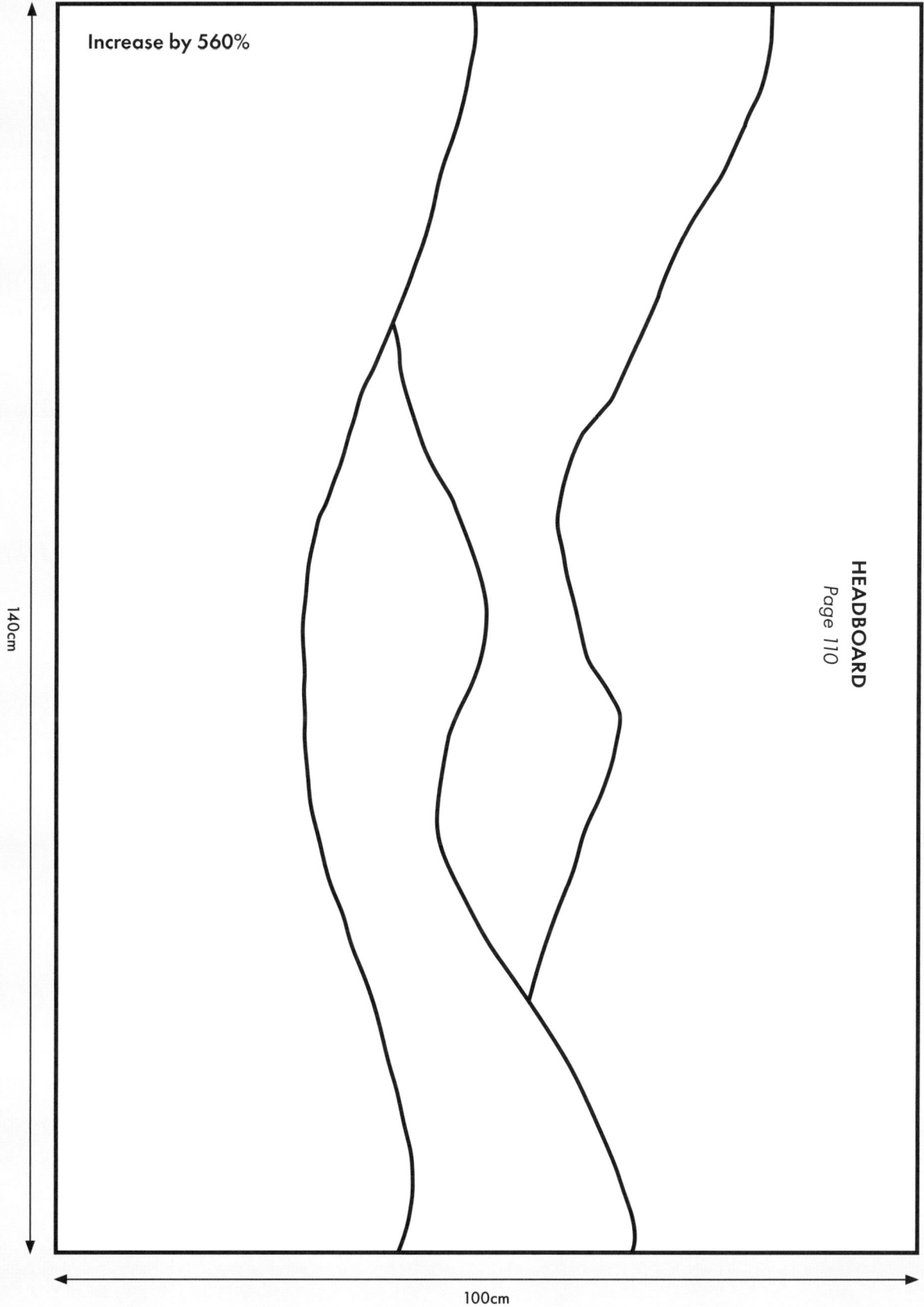

Increase by 560%

140cm

100cm

HEADBOARD
Page 110

resources

With fibre arts and crafts gaining popularity, there are more quality materials available on the market than ever. I encourage you to shop local and support small businesses. There's nothing like the excitement of walking into a yarn or haberdashery shop and getting to feel and touch a variety of different fibres.

PEG LOOMS
Dales Looms - UK
www.daleslooms.co.uk

Pukka Pacas - UK
www.pukkapacas.com

The Woolery - US
www.woolery.com

Dewberry Ridge - US
www.dewberryridge.com

G & M Peg Looms Beltrum - Netherlands
www.peglooms.nl

WEAVING STICKS
Wooden Weaving Sticks - Clover weaving sticks - US
www.clover-usa.com

Metal Weaving Sticks - Daegrad on Etsy - UK
www.etsy.com/uk/shop/Daegrad

ADDITIONAL MATERIALS
Wooden Dowels - Plug it - UK
www.plugitwood.co.uk

Basket Wooden Base - Fred Aldous - UK
www.fredaldous.co.uk

Flexi-Frame for Pouch - by Prym - UK
www.sewessential.co.uk

YARNS
Your local yarn shop.

World of Wool
www.worldofwool.co.uk

Wool and the Gang
www.woolandthegang.com

Hobbycraft (rope) - UK
www.hobbycraft.co.uk

Airedale Yarns (Dreadlock Wool) - UK
www.airedaleyarns.co.uk

Bobbiny (Jumbo 9mm Cord) - Europe
www.shop.bobbiny.com/en

about the author

Stephanie Fradette is the fibre artist behind the brand 'Le Petit Moose', a nod to her French-Canadian roots. The Scottish-based yarn enthusiast and designer-maker incorporates bold and contrasting colours throughout her woven collections, showcasing rich textures and contemporary design. Using a variety of techniques, she draws on structural and layered horizons often inspired by the ever-changing coastal landscapes from her world travels. She has been weaving since 2014, collaborated with Mollie Makes and enjoys delivering community-building creative workshops across the UK.

When she is not busy in her garden studio surrounded by wool, Stephanie can be found with her head in a novel, mastering the mystical art of the coffee bean, or dreaming about her next adventure on the seaside.

www.lepetitmoose.com @lepetitmoose

Acknowledgements I would like to give an enormous THANK YOU to everyone that has supported me in this monumental endeavor and passion project. To all the workshop students over the years, thank you for feeding my purpose and desire to transfer my love for fibre arts and all the wonderful opportunities and connections it has provided me with – I couldn't have done it without your support. Thank you to Katherine Raderecht who has wholeheartedly trusted me with this project. To Charlotte and the team at Pen & Sword and White Owl books for your patience, help and guidance. To Lisa Comfort for letting us use your beautiful home for the shoot. To Jesse Wild for making the projects shine in a new light with your keen photographic eye. Thank you to Jane Toft and Laura Bremner for bringing the playful design to the pages. To my two wonderful girls Sienna and Eva, I promise not to take over your playroom with yarn anymore (unless you want me to!). To Simon for your eternal support for all my projects, big and small plus making sense of my words. 'Un gros merci' to my crafty mother for igniting my creative spark at such a young age. And last, but not least, thank you to all my friends and global family who have supported me near and far, by your encouraging words, listening ear and enthusiasm. I can't wait to see you all again to share good food, laugh face–to–face and get creative together.